THE PENGUIN CLASSICS

FOUNDER EDITOR (1944–64): E. V. RIEU

PRESENT EDITORS:
Betty Radice and Robert Baldick

L212

ALEXANDER O. EXQUEMELIN was born in about 1645 of uncertain nationality, but it is likely that he was a native of Harfleur in France, who on his return from buccaneering settled in Holland. In 1666 he went with the French West India Company to Tortuga; he served there for three years before enlisting with the buccaneers, with whom he served until 1674, presumably as barber-surgeon, and then returned to Europe. In 1697 he acted as a surgeon during the attack on Cartagena. This book, originally published in Dutch as *De Americaensche Zee-Roovers*, first appeared in 1678. Exquemelin died after 1707.

ALEXIS BROWN was born in Shropshire and, after living abroad for many years in the Balearics, Morocco and the Canary Islands, she has now returned to England. She is the author of several books for children and *Three Years Long, A Valley Wide*, an account of the changing life in a remote Spanish village. Her translations from the Dutch include *Little King, Big King*, a play by Ben Minoli, *A Flower for Tomorrow* by A. Koolhaas, and various books on art, history and technical subjects.

A. O. EXQUEMELIN

The Buccaneers of America

*

TRANSLATED FROM THE DUTCH BY
ALEXIS BROWN

WITH AN INTRODUCTION BY
JACK BEECHING

PENGUIN BOOKS
BALTIMORE · MARYLAND

Penguin Books Ltd, Harmondsworth, Middlesex, England
Penguin Books Inc., 7110 Ambassador Court, Baltimore, Maryland 21207, U.S.A.
Penguin Books Australia Ltd, Ringwood, Victoria, Australia

—

This translation published 1969

—

Copyright © Alexis Brown, 1969

—

Introduction copyright © Jack Beeching, 1969

—

Made and printed in Great Britain
by Richard Clay (The Chaucer Press) Ltd.,
Bungay, Suffolk
Set in Monotype Garamond

CONTENTS

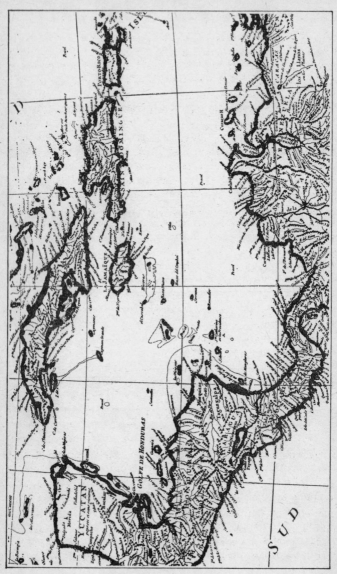

The islands and land areas chiefly involved in the narrative
(from Charlevoix' Histoire de l'Isle Espagnole ou de S. Domingue, Paris, 1732)

INTRODUCTION

THE Spaniards, in their greatest days, never cared overmuch for the ungentlemanly business of buying cheap and selling dear. Such articles as a *caballero*'s landed estate might be deficient in, gold would buy – and year after year, from their new American possessions, gold arrived by the ton. As manufacture in Spain itself decayed from neglect, this American gold went abroad to buy common necessities there; and thus, in the process of trade, a great deal of it, which thousands of enslaved Indians had died under the whip to mine and smelt, ended up in the strong-boxes of heretic merchants north of the Pyrenees. These were Spain's rivals, Dutch, French and English, pushing out in their trading-ships to the four quarters of the globe, to establish a world market.

In Spain's American provinces, trade was rigorously controlled. No Spanish American might, for instance, work as a dyer, a weaver, a fuller, a shoemaker or a hatter; and all commerce across the Atlantic had to go, by official convoy, to the inconvenient port of Seville. Yet tropical produce from Spanish America could be traded easily enough on the open European market, and the proceeds go to buy the simple manufactures that were necessary in every *hacienda*.

So Madrid's attempt to seal off her oversea possessions from world trade inevitably broke down. Trading countries could find off-shore bases in the Caribbean merely for the taking, because the *conquistadores* after 1540 had begun to make for the mainland, and settle in Mexico and Peru. As early as 1607 the English were established in St Kitts, and by the time the French took Guadeloupe and the Dutch Curaçao, Spain's European competitors had arrived on her imperial doorstep, to stay.

Spanish planters came half-way to meet these interlopers. A sloop would be run at night into some lonely American

7

estuary, or a trading-ship enter a harbour there under the pretext of storm damage, and carry on an illicit trade winked at by high officials who, having paid heavily for their posts in Madrid, were glad of a bribe. This clandestine trade, as years went by, gave English, French and Dutch seamen a thorough knowledge of the Latin American coast, and their ships, plying in the Caribbean, were at the service of ambitious European powers in time of war. Any trader who wished could then take a privateer's commission, and prey for a change upon Spanish coastal shipping. War, indeed, often continued in the Caribbean after peace had been declared in Europe, and seamen at the time had a saying, 'No peace beyond the line' – meaning a line drawn on their charts, west of the Azores and north of Capricorn.

The most dazzling prize was one of the treasure fleets, which sailed annually to Seville from designated ports in Mexico and along the Spanish Main. The Dutch West India Company, for instance, paid its shareholders in 1628 a dividend of fifty per cent from the proceeds of a single plate ship, captured out of Vera Cruz. But humdrum commerce was profitable, too. By the end of the seventeenth century, of all the manufactures consumed in Spain itself, an estimated five-sixths were being supplied by foreigners; and contraband accounted for nine-tenths of all trade with South America. There was, moreover, a growing tendency for Spanish colonists to turn their backs on the sea, even to move entire towns inland, since an unfamiliar sail off shore nowadays began to signify, not a useful cargo of trade goods or African slaves, but the advent of 'Protestant pirates' – *los corsarios luteranos* – who, as buccaneering developed, would come ashore simply to burn and plunder.

*

Spain, by working the Caribs to death, managed to depopulate the large island of Hispaniola (now shared between Haiti and Santo Domingo). The northern shore had never been properly settled, and by 1600 vast herds could be found there, the progeny of hogs and cattle that had run wild in the forest ever since *haciendas* farther to the south were abandoned.

Traders crossing the Atlantic – at the time chiefly Dutch – were always ready to exchange gunpowder, cloth or brandy for ship's victuals for their return trip, as well as to take on a cargo of hides and tallow, so there was a livelihood to be made in northern Hispaniola by hunting. From about 1610 onward, a number of masterless men from many parts of Europe took refuge there, in the forest. They comprised sailors who had jumped ship or escaped from a wreck, and the debris of extreme Protestant sects dispersed by Europe's religious wars, and later were joined by runaway bonded servants, then being shipped out from Europe under service contracts that verged on slavery, as tobacco plantations in the newly occupied West Indian islands began to cry out for labour. These men, until Colbert's colonizing policy eventually brought out French Catholics to join them, were fiercely Protestant as well as aggressively anti-Spanish.

They got the nickname 'buccaneer' because of a method they learned from the surviving Carib Indians for smoke-drying beef, which became their stock-in-trade. The meat was hung in strips over a frame of green sticks, and dried above a fire fed with animal bones and hide trimmings. Both the wooden grating and the place where the curing was done were called by the Carib name of *boucan*, and the hunters engaged in this work became known as *boucaniers*.

Sailors then believed that all previous obligations were wiped out the moment a man 'passed the Tropic'. In the forests of Hispaniola the buccaneers began to evolve their own code – the Custom of the Coast – transferring to it such obedience as they had hitherto owed to the laws of the different European nations which they had left behind. They would abide strictly by these customary rules, even in every-day matters. No one, for instance, on a hunting trip would eat a mouthful of food until as many beasts had been killed that day as there were hunters in the company. Their code covered all the eventualities of life, and was enforced by duelling and boycott.

This little community of professional hunters, several times broken up by Spanish punitive expeditions, only to reappear in response to an irresistible economic demand, moved in about 1630 to a rocky, turtle-shaped and more defensible off-shore island called Tortuga. The Spaniards, as a final measure, then tried to get rid of the buccaneers by systematically destroying the wild herds on which they lived, but this only drove more of them into the alternative mode of life that offered, piracy. Later in the century, as Exquemelin describes, though these men still plant and hunt, the Custom of the Coast now details how the proceeds of piracy shall be fairly and justly divided, and the buccaneers have progressed from simple attacks on Spanish coastal vessels to large-scale raids on fortified mainland towns.

At first, they took to the sea in dug-out canoes. Armed only with pistol, cutlass and musket, the buccaneers would boldly attack a large sailing-ship mounting cannon. The buccaneers shot with the accuracy of professional hunters – they were able, with their long-barrelled muzzle-loaders, to hit a coin spinning in mid-air – and their tactical rule of thumb was that four muskets were as good as one big gun. Later on, they went out in single-masted barques with a leg-of-mutton sail – the best were of cedar from Bermuda – or two-masted barquentines, with one mast square-rigged.

These ships were of shallow draught, enabling the buccaneers to lurk in coastal shoals along the Bay of Honduras, as well as to patrol the channels between Hispaniola, Puerto Rico, Cuba and the mainland peninsula of Yucatan. A glance at the map will show how they could thus take their toll of all Spanish shipping coming north for Mexico, Florida or Europe. Since fire-power in the moment of attack was so important to the buccaneers, they developed a habit of crowding as many fighting men into a ship as she would carry, so that when food ran low, as it commonly did, they attacked their prey under the double provocation of greed and physical hunger.

The buccaneers marred their spectacular courage against

disproportionate odds by a meditated cruelty* that was
excessive even for a policy of terror. This morbid taste of
theirs for inflicting pain perhaps followed, psychologically,
not only from their lust for plunder – their obsessive thing-
worship – but also from the unusual society they had evolved:
celibate, with its origins in the fo'c'sle, and its own peculiar
institution of *matelotage*, touched on briefly here by Exquemelin. There had, of course, been military societies with
homosexual overtones before – Sacred Legion, Templars,
Samurai – and arguably, in those early years, before the
French colonizers shipped out the first cargo of women to
Tortuga, the buccaneers formed such another, and their
extreme cruelty was a function of the way they lived together.

*

The buccaneers were still on their way to containing Spanish
attacks on their settlement, and might even, as more run-
aways joined them, have evolved in time a new, free-enter-
prise, multi-national little American republic, a century
before the Declaration of Independence. But they fought too
well; they were too valuable at sea and on land as auxiliaries
in time of war. Step by step the buccaneers were induced to
quit their perilously unbridled life of hunting and piracy, for
the advantages of a well defended harbour under some
European flag, where they could readily sell off their plunder,
and spend the cash proceeds in spectacular debauch. It paid
handsomely to patronize the buccaneers, and so, from the
middle of the seventeenth century onwards, their ships often
went cruising nominally as English and French privateers.

*As to their cruelty, Exquemelin is not our only witness. Thus John
Style writes to the Secretary of State (Colonial State Papers, 1669, 74,
no. 138): 'It is a common thing among the privateers . . . to cut a man in
pieces, first some flesh, then a hand, an arm, a leg, sometimes tying a
cord about his head, and with a stick twisting it until the eyes shoot out,
which is called "woolding". Before taking Porto Bello . . . a woman
there was set bare upon a baking stone, and roasted, because she did not
confess of money which she had only in their conceit; this he heard some
confess with boasting, and one that was sick confess with sorrow.'

Once the French, in the way Exquemelin describes, had slowly and tactfully established their own government on Tortuga, English buccaneers found themselves no longer popular there, and shifted to Jamaica, which an expeditionary force sent out by Cromwell had captured in 1655 and hurriedly populated by shipping out 4,500 whites, mostly under duress, and 1,500 Negro slaves. Since their ships were nearly all the defence the vulnerable new colony could look to, the buccaneers were heartily welcome, and Port Royal, Jamaica, soon became 'the wickedest city on earth'.

Even after the French and English buccaneers had thus allowed themselves to become cat's-paws of their respective governments, they still made joint filibustering expeditions, their usual rendezvous being Isla de la Vaca, midway between Port Royal and Tortuga. But the old-style Protestant solidarity was fast disappearing, and the bloodstained garb of the original buccaneer being laid aside. Some of the English who marched with Morgan across Panama wore faded red coats, from stores in Jamaica, which at one time had been uniform for the New Model Army; and, for their part, recent French Catholic recruits to buccaneering, who had mass said on board and sometimes gave a share of their plunder to the church, were horrified at the way the heretic English would loot altars, and use sacred images for target practice.

The days were over when the most respectable bond uniting the buccaneers had been religious, and Protestantism gave a distinctive moral sanction to the plunder of Catholic Spain. (This had been a supra-national loyalty that cut both ways. One Spanish attack on Tortuga was led by an Irish Catholic named Murphy. Another Irishman, Philip Fitzgerald, sailed a twelve-gun man-of-war out of Havana, and hanged any Protestants, preferably English, he could catch.) In the Caribbean, as in Europe, modern nationalism was victoriously asserting itself.

*

By 1677 it had been made a felony for an English buccaneer to serve under the French; and in 1683 buccaneering was forbidden, on pain of flogging and confiscation, even in Tortuga. For a while Adolf Esmit, the Danish governor of St Thomas, and a retired buccaneer himself, continued to give letters-of-marque, but he was able to protect his colony there, mostly English, no later than 1684. The capture of Cartagena in 1697 was the last time buccaneers were used as a naval auxiliary.

France and England were now well established in the West Indies. English colonies had been formally conceded by Spain in 1670, and the French royal house had hopes of legally inheriting the Spanish throne. Buccaneering undermined the confidence needed for the contraband trade; and since Spain might always take reprisals against foreign merchants in her home ports, it could be bad for trade in Europe, too. Moreover, white bond-slaves now had the option of escaping to join the buccaneers, a fact of which the larger plantation owners were no doubt aware when they officially and generously encouraged the buccaneers on Jamaica to retire and turn planter. The destruction by earthquake in 1692 of the wicked city of Port Royal symbolized the end, and the Peace of Ryswick in 1697 finally took the wind out of the buccaneers' sails. Some turned to downright piracy, and found new bases northward in the Bahamas and Carolina, and eastward in Madagascar.

The harm done through those inordinate years, when the peaceful and pious Spanish colonists were burned out of their homes, stripped of their property and tortured for ransom, can hardly be reduced to figures. But, at a cautious estimate, in their heyday between 1655 and 1671, the buccaneers sacked eighteen cities, four towns and thirty-five villages, quite apart from the immense damage they inflicted on seaborne trade. The Marques de Barina in 1685 estimated (possibly over-estimated) Spain's losses to the buccaneers since 1660 as having amounted to 60,000,000 crowns. All this gold, melted down into ingots and carefully preserved, is no doubt still in the vaults of some respectable banking establishment or other.

Very little of all this money stuck to the fingers of the buccaneers themselves, unless they happened to be such uncommon personalities as Henry Morgan, who clambered right up the ladder of conventional success, or de Lussan, an impoverished French gentleman, who made an expedition to Panama in 1684, when buccaneering was at its last gasp. He got back to France with enough money to set up in style again and write his memoirs – but it had all been won from his less provident and expert companions, at dice and cards. Most of the men who ravaged the Spanish Main spent their plunder quickly, in furious debauch, and at once put to sea for more, like frenzied victims of some contemporary infection, a gold-fetishism, a thing-fever.

*

Henry Morgan, who dominates this final phase and cuts an important figure in Exquemelin's narrative, was not so much one of the true breed of buccaneer as an unscrupulously able man, well connected socially, who knew how to turn buccaneering to his own advantage. His raids were the most spectacular and the best-documented; Exquemelin was present as an eyewitness, at least at the sack of Panama (though Morgan went so far as to sue his English publishers for libel; there were incidents earlier in his career that by then Henry Morgan preferred to keep obscure).

Morgan was born in 1635 at Llanrhymney, Glamorgan, of parents who evidently were prosperous yeomen, hopeful of one day being considered gentry. One uncle, Thomas Morgan, became General Monk's second-in-command, and served as governor of the island of Jersey. Another uncle, Colonel Edward Morgan, who happened in the Civil War to have taken the royalist side, went into exile in the Caribbean, and became a soldier once more, in Jamaica.

Morgan himself vigorously denied, later on, that he had ever been an indentured servant, though under the Commonwealth he might well have been transported to Jamaica against his will – thousands were, for no worse crime than being Irish, or Scots, or unemployed. Possibly, however, he sailed in 1654 with Penn and Venables, and would therefore have been nineteen at the time of their successful attack on Jamaica, when the buccaneers took the brunt of the sea-fighting.

Eleven years later, in the Second Dutch War of 1665, Morgan emerges as the owner of a sea-going ship, bought on the proceeds, there can be little doubt, of buccaneering, since already he had the prestige among the Brotherhood of the Coast to be acceptable as second-in-command to the outstanding buccaneer commander of that time, Edward Mansfield. (Exquemelin, who perhaps knew of Mansfield only by hearsay, gets his name and nationality wrong. He was English, or possibly Scots.)

Morgan prudently married his cousin, Colonel Edward Morgan's heiress, and emerged after Mansfield's death as the kingpin in Jamaican naval strategy – the one personality the government could rely on to cajole and command the buccaneers in the interest of English colonial policy.

Sir Thomas Modyford, governor of Jamaica and a crony of Morgan's, was a man who had been in the West Indies since 1650. He understood both the naval role of buccaneering and the hard cash to be made out of it, and issued the buccaneers, who already were well accustomed to operating as a fleet, with letters-of-marque in his own name. He judged that audacious and unnerving raids on near-by Spanish possessions, as well as showing a cash profit, would be the infant colony's best defence, so he gave Morgan a free hand.

In 1668, at the age of thirty-three, Morgan captured Porto Bello, his official report on the action – which might reach London – being a masterpiece of soft soap. In March 1669 he sacked Maracaibo – and when deploring, as one must, the beastly cruelties of his followers there, one must also bear in mind that both King Charles II, as monarch, and his brother James, as Lord High Admiral, took their official percentage of the bloodstained plunder.

In May of the same year, when London yielded to Spanish protests, Modyford was obliged to call in all privateering commissions, but in the year following, a Spanish attack on the undefended north shore of Jamaica gave Morgan and Modyford their pretext for a reprisal on the largest (and most profitable) scale. The more accessible Spanish cities had already been plundered so often that returns were diminishing. On 14 August of that year, Morgan opened a new buccaneering epoch when, with official connivance, he marched across the Isthmus to the Pacific coast, and sacked Panama.

Since the days of Drake, the western coast of Latin America had been relatively unmolested; with Morgan's attack on Panama the powers hostile to Spain re-entered the Pacific. But Morgan checked his men forcibly when they would have taken ship from Panama to carry buccaneering all the way down the coast – since, unlike them, he had to consider the political repercussions of such an extended seaborne raid.

Whether Morgan had his men set Panama on fire is a debatable question, and may hinge, too, on his need to control the buccaneers, since making Panama inhospitable to them as a base would encourage them to return with him across the Isthmus. Exquemelin, a witness of truth except for his vagueness about numbers and dates, is emphatic that Morgan did fire Panama. Sir William Godolphin, however, writing from Madrid to Lord Arlington, Secretary of State, says the president of Panama himself had left orders that the city, if taken, should be fired. (Though this, no doubt, is what an English diplomat so placed would have been glad for Madrid to believe.)

There is a similar conflict of opinion over the episode of Morgan and his beautiful Spanish prisoner. Richard Browne, surgeon-general to the fleet, and one of those witnesses a commander-in-chief would be grateful for at any hostile court of inquiry, states categorically, 'As to their women, I know not or ever heard of anything offered beyond their wills . . . as for the Admiral, he was noble enough to the vanquished enemy,' but this statement, if taken at its face value, contradicts not only Exquemelin but everything else we know about the buccaneers' behaviour towards the other sex. The fact was that Morgan and Modyford, in using irregular troops of practised cruelty, were inevitably driven to whitewash their actions afterwards.

The sack of Panama – when Morgan cheated his followers of the share reserved to them by custom – demonstrated that the Pacific coast was wide open, even if the traditional buccaneer code might have gone by the board. We know something of what happened on later raids across the Isthmus, made by Captain Sharp and others, since there are interesting accounts in the buccaneer journals collected by Sir Hans Sloane, and later acquired by the British Museum. Though scrappy, compared to Exquemelin's narrative, they bear out in an occasional vivid detail his picture of buccaneering.

Sir Hans, who saw Morgan when he was fifty-three, describes him, clinically, as 'lean, sallow-coloured, eyes a little prominent, belly jutting out'. But by then, much else had happened in Morgan's career. Arrested and sent back to England in a warship, as a sop to the enraged Spaniards, he had nevertheless been made much of at the court of Charles II, where ready money and a certain brutal dash went a long way. In 1675 Sir Henry Morgan returned to Jamaica as deputy governor.

*

About Exquemelin himself there are certain questions that scarcely yield to conjecture.

His book, *De Americaensche Zee-Roovers*, a quarto with handsome cuts, now extremely rare, was first published in Dutch by Jan ten Hoorn of Amsterdam, in 1678. A German translation, *Americanische Seeraüber*, followed in 1679, and in 1681 a Spanish edition appeared as *Piratas de la America*. It had been translated by Dr Alonso de Buena-Maison, a medical man who also lived in Amsterdam.

The first English translation, published by W. Crook, London, 1684, entitled *Bucaniers of America* (with the author's name anglicized to Esquemeling), derives from this Spanish version. In the same year an entirely distinct English edition, entitled *The History of the Bucaniers*, was published by Thomas Malthus. These were the two English publications involved in Morgan's libel case. He sued Crook and Malthus for £10,000, and recovered £200 from each, with damages. More to the point, both publishers made apologies, and amended later editions, Malthus declaring that the 'filth and ordure' of the Spanish version had 'now been cleared away'. This Penguin Classic edition is the first translation accurately based on the Dutch ever to appear in English.

In 1686 the Sieur de Frontignières published in Paris a French version in two volumes, twelvemo, entitled *Histoire des Aventuriers*. It includes information about the Spanish West Indies found in the first Dutch edition but later omitted, and expands the account of life on Tortuga, but cautiously omits details which in France might have caused political offence. The editor, who sounds well informed, says the author was a Frenchman called Oexmelin, from Harfleur.

If this were so, why should he write in Dutch? Assuming, however, that the original document might have been the journal of a French eyewitness called Oexmelin – then whose hand turned it into Dutch?

It must again be stressed that where Exquemelin's facts may be checked from State Papers or independent witnesses they tally, but for such minor lapses as have already been noted. He was clearly an intelligent, thoughtful, accurately observing man, who took part personally in many of the events he describes. An outline of his life may be hazarded.

He was born about 1645, and must have died after 1707. In 1666 he went (a Frenchman? a Breton? Flemish? Dutch?) to Tortuga, as an *engagé* of the French West India Company. He served there three years and then enlisted with the buccaneers, this being at a time in Tortuga when, though retaining much of their independence, they had begun on occasion to serve French interests at sea. He served until 1674, presumably as barber-surgeon, and then returned to Europe. In the attack on Cartagena in 1697, which was the buccaneers' swan-song, he makes an appearance on the muster-roll as a surgeon.

A theory that for a long time found favour was that Exquemelin might be the pseudonym of a Dutch author, Hendrick Barentzoon Smeeks, who in 1708 published with ten Hoorn a romance called *Krinke Kesmes*, about being cast away on the shores of Australia, based on his own experiences. Smeeks was in the service of the Dutch East India Company until 1665, returned to Holland in 1673, where he was assistant-surgeon in the home fleet, settled in Zwolle as a surgeon in 1680 and died in 1721. Between the years of 1666 and 1672 he served as surgeon to the French West India Company. Smeeks, when writing of the buccaneers, might reasonably (might he not?) have chosen to hide his identity behind the name of a non-Dutch brother surgeon known to have sailed with them, thereby keeping this discreditable aspect of his own past from the knowledge of his respectable burgher patients.

But, in 1934, M. Vriejman found the names of both Exquemelin (1679) and Smeeken [*sic*] (1666) on the books of the Dutch Surgeons' Guild, as having passed their qualifying examinations. Exquemelin, therefore, on his return from the West Indies, went to Amsterdam to qualify professionally, and must have been living there while the history that bears his name was written and published. The 'pseudonym' theory will not hold water. But as Latin was still the academic lingua franca, why need Exquemelin, even though he qualified in Amsterdam, have learnt Dutch so quickly and well? And why write his book in it, if he had French at his command?

The most probable view, perhaps, on the information we have, is that Exquemelin was originally Oexmelin and a native of Harfleur, but that on his return from buccaneering he chose to settle in Holland, possibly because he was a Huguenot. His journal could have been worked up there for the publisher, ten Hoorn, with the aid of another surgeon who perhaps was his old acquaintance, Hendrick Smeeks, and shortly thereafter translated into Spanish by a third Amsterdam medical man of literary tastes, de Buena-Maison. But this is guesswork.

Exquemelin, anyway, wrote a contemporary best-seller, reprinted at steady intervals down to our own day and the principal source of our knowledge about the buccaneers. His colourful personal recollections coincided with the taste then developing in Europe for the lowlife picaresque, and so the buccaneer has become established as a stock figure in our romantic mythology. Anarchistic, untrammelled, extravagant, sadistic, a crack shot and wildly courageous, the buccaneer is the gay dog among Protestant paladins – not only a fantasy figure for today's cautiously ethical businessman, but his exact historical progenitor.

JACK BEECHING

THE BUCCANEERS OF AMERICA

Comprising a pertinent and truthful description
of the principal acts of depredation and inhuman
cruelty committed by the English and French
buccaneers against the Spaniards
in America.

IN THREE PARTS:

PART ONE

How the French came to Hispaniola;
the nature of the country
and life of the inhabitants.

PART TWO

The origin of the buccaneers;
their rules and way of life;
various attacks on the Spaniards.

PART THREE

The burning of Panama City
by the English and French buccaneers,
together with an account of
a further voyage by the author.

WRITTEN BY

A. O. EXQUEMELIN

who himself, of necessity, was present
at all these acts of plunder.

PART ONE

*How the French came to Hispaniola;
the nature of the country
and life of the inhabitants.*

*

The Gulf of Venezuela and Lake Maracaibo
(*from Charlevoix' Histoire de l'Isle Espagnole ou de S. Domingue, Paris, 1732*)

CHAPTER ONE

*The author's departure for the western part of
America, in the service of the French West India
Company. Encounter at sea with an English
warship. Arrival at the island of Tortuga.*

IN the year 1666, on the second of May, we left Havre de
Grace in the *St John*, under the direction of the West India
Company's delegate. The ship mounted twenty-eight guns
and carried twenty seamen and two hundred and twenty
passengers, including indentured servants of the Company
and free persons with their servants.

We came to anchor below the Cape of Barfleur, in order to
meet with seven more of the Company's ships due to arrive
from Dieppe, together with a warship mounting thirty-seven
guns and two hundred and fifty men.

Two ships were bound for Senegal, five for the Caribbean
Islands, and ourselves for the island of Tortuga. Some twenty
vessels bound for Newfoundland also joined us, along with a
few Dutch ships making for La Rochelle, Nantes and St
Martin. Altogether, we formed a fleet of about thirty ships,
and at once we made ready for action, as we feared four
English frigates (each of sixty guns) were cruising around the
Isle of Ornay, in wait for us.

After our commodore, the Chevalier de Sourdis, had given
his orders, we got under sail with a good wind, in foggy
weather. This favoured us, as the English might not spot us,
and we hugged the French coast in order to elude the enemy.
We encountered a Flemish ship from Ostend, which complained to our commodore it had been plundered that very
morning by a French corsair. The warship gave chase
directly, but was unable to overtake the pirate. The French
peasants were in alarm all along the coast, thinking we were

English and intending to land. We showed our flags, but they put no trust in them.

After this, we dropped anchor in the roadstead of Conquet in Brittany (near the Isle of Ushant) to take on provisions and fresh water. Supplied with all we needed, we continued our voyage, passing by way of the Raz de Fonteneau, as we dare not approach the Sorlingues because of the English cruisers. This Race, as its name implies, is a strong and rapid current, flowing over many rocks. It is situated close to the French coast, latitude 48° 10′ north, and is a very dangerous passage on account of the reefs, some lying submerged and some showing above water. By way of celebration, all those on our ship who had never previously made the passage were baptized in the following manner.

The bos'n of the ship dresses himself up in a long robe, with an outlandish cap on his head, a wooden sword in his right hand and a pot of blacking in his left. His face is daubed with black, and round his neck he wears a garland of blocks and other ship's tackle. Everyone who has never passed this way before has to kneel in front of him. He makes a cross on their forehead and gives them a blow on the nape of the neck with his wooden sword, and then they have water flung over them by the other bystanders. What is more, they must put a bottle of wine or brandy by the mainmast, but those who haven't any are excused. If the ship has never made the passage before, then the captain has to pay up. Afterwards, the wine and brandy found by the mast are shared out in the fo'c'sle.

The Dutchmen too used to have a baptism on passing these rocks, and also the rocks known as Berlingues which lie close to the coast of Portugal, 39° 40′ north. These reefs are extremely dangerous, for they cannot easily be seen at night on account of the high coastline. The Dutchmen have a completely different ceremony from the French, for when anyone is being baptized, he has to fall three times from the mainyard into the water, like a criminal, and if those on board are agreeable, they tow him behind the ship. It is a great honour to fall yet another time for His Highness, or for the captain's credit. The first who drops has a gun fired in his honour and the flag waved.

Anyone not willing to fall is bound, according to their laws, to give a shilling, and if he's an officer, he must pay two. Any passengers who refuse the baptism have to pay as much as they think fit. If the ship has never passed that way before, the captain has to give a hogshead of wine or else they saw off the roundhouse from the ship, and the captain can make no claim on that account. All the proceeds are given into the bos'n's hands until they get to port, where wine is bought and shared out among the whole ship's company in the fo'c'sle.

Nobody from either nation can give the reasons for doing these things, apart from its being an old custom among seamen. Some say the matter was so ordained by the Emperor Charles V, but it is not to be found in his book of laws. Having in passing described these ceremonies of the sailors, we will now continue our voyage.

When we had passed the Race, we got a favourable wind until Cape Finisterre, where we met with a very heavy storm which scattered us from each other. This storm lasted eight days. It was wretched to see how the people on our ship were slopped about from port to starboard, and had not the heart to stand upright, they were so seasick; the sailors had to step over them to do their work. Afterwards we had calm weather and followed our course, passing below the Tropic of Cancer. This is a circle imagined by the star-gazers, marking the limit of the sun towards the north, and lies 23° 30′ north of the Line. There we were again baptized in the manner I have described above – for the French always hold a baptism at this point, and on crossing the Line, and at the Tropic of Capricorn south of the Line. We had a favourable wind, which we badly needed, for we were running short of water, being each rationed to a pint and a half a day.

About the latitude of Barbados, we caught sight of an English naval vessel, which gave chase, but seeing he had no advantage on us, he drew off. We pursued him, firing on him with our eight-pounders, but he was better rigged, so we had to let him go. We then resumed our course, and the island of Martinique came in sight. We did all we could to reach the roadstead of St Peter, but were prevented by a strong current. We then made for Guadeloupe, but neither could we reach this shore on account of the current, so we carried on towards the island of Tortuga, which was our destination.

We passed along the coast of Puerto Rico, an extremely lovely and pleasant island, covered with beautiful trees up to the tops of the mountains. The island of Hispaniola, which we shall describe later on, then came in view. We sailed along the coast until at last we arrived at Tortuga, on the seventh of July of the same year, without having lost a man on the whole voyage. The Company's goods were unloaded here, and the ship proceeded to Cul de Sac, taking those passengers who had to go there.

CHAPTER TWO

*Description of the Island of Tortuga: its plants
and fruits. How the French came there, and were
twice driven out by the Spaniards. How the author
came to be sold on two occasions.*

TORTUGA lies on the north side of the great and renowned
island of Hispaniola, about three leagues from the coast,
20° 30′ north. The small island is some sixteen leagues in
circumference, and acquired its name because its shape is
like a turtle, which the Spanish call 'tortuga'. Although extremely rocky, it is covered with large trees, which grow
where no soil can be seen, with their roots lying naked on the
rocks. The north side is uninhabited and most inhospitable,
having neither harbour nor beaches, apart from a few gaps
between the crags. People live only on the south side, and
here there is but one harbour which ships can enter.

The inhabited portion is divided into four parts, of which
the Low Country is the most important, on account of the
port. This is reasonably good and unimpeded by a reef;
there are two channels to sail in by. Ships of seventy guns can
enter, and the harbour has a very clear sandy bottom. The
town is called Cayona and is where the principal planters live.
The Middle Plantation is a region recently cultivated, and is
very rich in tobacco, as is the district called La Ringot; both
these places lie to the west of the island. The Mountain is the
region where the first plantations were made.

As for the vegetation, some excellent timber grows on
Tortuga, including fustic [a wood which yields a yellow dye]
and red, white and yellow sandalwood. The inhabitants call
the yellow sort *bois de chandelle*, or candlewood, because it will
burn as bright as a candle, and serves for making torches with
which to go fishing at night. Another tree which grows here

is the *lignum sanctum* – known in these parts as pox-wood. There are many of the trees which provide *gummi elemi*, and also *radix chinae* or China-root, but this is not so good as the East Indian variety; it is very white and soft, and is eaten by the wild pigs,

As well as timber, much sought after for building ships and houses, aloes and many other medicinal herbs and shrubs grow here. All sorts of fruits and plants are found, similar to those on the Caribbean Islands. They include manioc, sweet potatoes, yams, melons and water-melons, guavas, bananas and plantains, pineapples, cashew-nuts, and many others which I will not weary the reader by listing. There is also an abundance of palm trees, from which wine is made, and the leaves are used for covering the houses.

There are many wild boar, but hunting them with dogs is forbidden lest they be exterminated, as the island is so small. Should enemies attack, the people could then retire to the woods and live by hunting. Nevertheless, hunting is very dangerous: the crags are often covered with scrub and a man could fall down a concealed precipice unawares. Various people have been lost in this manner. Numerous skeletons have been found, but one could not judge whether the men had died recently or not.

At a certain time of the year, wild pigeons flock here in such multitudes the inhabitants could live on them alone, without using other meat. But when this season is past, they are no longer good to eat. They become thin and bitter to taste, because of a certain seed they eat, which is bitter in the extreme.

Many sea-crabs and land-crabs are found on the shore. They are very large, and are edible. The slaves and indentured servants often eat them: their taste is good, but they are most harmful to the eyes. Frequent eating of them brings on a fit of giddiness, so that for perhaps a quarter of an hour one is unable to see.

Having settled colonies on the island of St Kitts and being reasonably strong there, the French equipped a number of vessels and steered westward to discover what they could, and so reached the coast of Hispaniola. On landing, they found it to be very fertile, abounding with all kinds of animals, such as wild bulls and cows, swine and horses. As they could make no profit out of them without having a refuge of some sort (since Hispaniola is well populated by the Spaniards) they decided to take Tortuga. This they did, chasing out some ten or twelve Spaniards who were living there. The French stayed there about half a year without anyone disturbing them. They made journeys in their canoes to and from the big island, and began making plantations on Tortuga, and sent for still more settlers.

Meanwhile, the Spaniards, unable to view this activity favourably, fitted out some ships and came to recapture Tortuga. This they succeeded in doing, for as soon as the French saw them coming, they fled with their goods to the forest, and crossed over to Hispaniola in their canoes at night. They had the advantage of not being encumbered with women and children, so everyone could take to the woods to hunt for food, and also give warning to the rest of their mates, so as to leave the Spaniards no time for building fortifications on Tortuga.

The Spaniards crossed back, intending to drive them out or make them die of hunger, as they had done with the Indians, but they had little success, for the French were well provided with powder, bullets and good fire-arms. Taking advantage of a time when most of the Spaniards had sailed back to the big island with their guns and many men to harry the French, these men returned once more to Tortuga. They drove out all the Spaniards who were still there, prevented the others from coming back again, and remained masters of the island.

Having won the island, the French sent for assistance, requesting the governor or general of St Kitts to send them a governor to establish better order among the people, and to found a colony there. The general, well pleased with the idea, immediately ordered a ship lying in the roads to make ready, and sent M. le Vasseur to be governor of Tortuga, together with many men and all kinds of necessaries.

On arrival, this governor had a fortress built on a rock, where it could protect the port from enemy ships. This fort is most difficult of access; it can be approached from one side only, by a way so narrow that no more than two people can enter at the same time. In the middle of the rock is a cave which serves as a storehouse for ammunition, and on top is a suitable site for raising a battery. The governor had a house built at the fort, and mounted two guns there, reached by climbing a ladder, which could be pulled up behind. Inside the fort is a spring of sweet water, fit to supply a thousand people daily – a supply which cannot be cut off, for it gushes out of the rocks. All around the fort are plantations, which are very rich in tobacco and other crops.

When the French had established their colony and made it reasonably strong, each man set about seeking his own fortune. Some crossed over to the big island to hunt and get hides. Others, who did not fancy such activity, took to marauding, privateering along the Spanish coast as they still do today. The rest, who had wives, stayed on the island, some making plantations and growing tobacco, others setting up taverns, so that everyone found the means of making his living.

The Spaniards could not look on this work with favourable eyes, judging the French would become so powerful that in the end they would turn them out of the big island. They seized the chance, when many of the French were at sea and others off hunting, to equip their canoes and land for the second time on Tortuga, with the assistance of some French prisoners they had with them. The Spaniards were 800 strong.

The French could not prevent their landing, and therefore withdrew to the fort. The governor had all the trees around the fort cut down in order to get a clearer view of the enemy. As there was no chance of forcing the stronghold without artillery, the Spaniards considered how best to set about it. They saw that only the tall trees sheltering the fort had been cut down, and that the place could be brought under fire from the mountain, so they made a road by which they could bring up ordnance to the top.

This mountain is quite high, and from the summit one can see the whole island all around. It is level on top, and surrounded with crags, making it inaccessible save by the track the Spaniards made, as I shall now relate.

The Spaniards had many slaves and labourers with them – *matates* or half-breeds and Indians. These they set to work making a road through the rocks and dragging artillery up the mountain, in order to mount a battery, fire on the fort where the French were, and force them to surrender. But while the Spaniards were busy with this undertaking, the French managed to warn their comrades to come to their aid, which they did. The hunters united with the men engaged in privateering, and, having landed on Tortuga by night, they succeeded in climbing the mountain from the north side, because they were familiar with the place.

The Spaniards had, with great difficulty, managed to get two cannon up the mountain ready to bombard the fort next day, and knew nothing of the arrival of the French. But next morning, just as the Spaniards were busy setting their cannon in order, the French attacked from the rear. Most of the Spaniards sprang headlong over the precipice, where they broke neck and legs, not one of them landing safely. The Frenchmen killed the rest, allowing no quarter. Hearing the shrieks, the other Spaniards down below judged that matters were going badly on the mountain-top. They went to the shore and at once put to sea, despairing of ever conquering Tortuga.

The governors of Tortuga always acted as proprietors of the island, until 1664, when the French West India Company took possession and installed M. d'Ogeron as governor. They settled a colony there, with their delegate and indentured servants, intending to carry on trade with the Spaniards, as the Dutch in Curaçao do. But this plan was not successful. They wanted to trade with a foreign nation, yet could not manage commerce with their own people. When the Company started up, everyone – privateers, hunters, planters and all – bought from them, for the Company supplied everything on credit. But when it came to paying, nobody was to be found. So the Company was obliged to send for its factors, ordering them to sell up everything which could be sold, and close down the enterprise.

All the indentured servants of the Company were sold, some for twenty pieces of eight and some for thirty. As a servant of the Company myself, I was among those sold, and had just the ill luck to fall into the hands of the wickedest rogue in the whole island. He was the deputy governor or lieutenant-general, and he did me all the harm he could think of. He even made me suffer intense hunger, depriving me of my food. He wanted me to buy my freedom for 300 pieces of eight, offering to let me go for that amount.

Finally, I fell into a severe illness through all the discomfort I'd been through, and my master, fearing I should die, sold me to a surgeon for seventy pieces of eight. When I began to recover my health, I had nothing to wear except an old shirt and a pair of drawers. My new master was considerably better than the first. He gave me clothes and everything I needed, and when I had served him a year he offered to set me free for 150 pieces of eight, agreeing to wait for payment until I had earned the money.

When I was free once more, I was like Adam when he was first created. I had nothing at all, and therefore resolved to join the privateers or buccaneers, with whom I stayed until the year 1670, accompanying them on their various voyages and taking part in many important raids, as I shall describe later on in this account. But first I will write something on the island of Hispaniola, to satisfy the reader's curiosity in everything worthy of note in the western part of America.

CHAPTER THREE

*Description of the great and celebrated island
of Hispaniola.*

HISPANIOLA lies between latitudes $17\frac{1}{2}°$ and $20°$ north, having a circumference of about 300 leagues. From east to west it extends 120 leagues, and is about fifty leagues in breadth, narrowing in some places. I shall not trouble the reader with recounting the discovery of this famous island, since everyone knows how, in the year 1492, Christopher Columbus was sent forth by Don Ferdinand, King of Spain, and discovered this island, from which time to the present the Spaniards have possessed it.

The Spaniards have built several cities there, and many pleasant villages. The capital is dedicated to St Dominic and is named after this saint – San Domingo in the Spanish tongue. This city is situated on the south coast, $18°$ $13'$ north, and lies some forty leagues from the eastern point, called Punta de Espada. It is a walled city, with a strong castle to protect the port. There is a fine harbour, where many ships can berth, being sheltered from all winds except the south. Around the city lie most beautiful plantations, where all kinds of fruits grow, according to the nature of the country.

The governor of the island, whom they call the president, resides there, and all the country towns and villages receive their supplies from this city, for the Spaniards trade at no other seaport. Most of the residents are merchants and shop-keepers.

The town of St Jago de los Caballeros is dedicated to St James, and is a country town without walls, lying at about $19°$ north. The inhabitants are for the most part hunters and planters. The place is well suited to such occupations: all around are lovely meadows abounding with wild and tame cattle, so that hides of good quality are obtained from these parts.

To the south of St Jago is a pleasant village called El Cotui, or Nuestra Señora de Alta Gracia – Our Lady of Grace. The rich farmlands around this village produce much cacao or chocolate, ginger and tobacco, and the cattle provide plenty of tallow.

Off the south coast is a small island called Savona, where the Spaniards often go to catch turtles, which come ashore to lay their eggs in the sand. Nothing worthy of description is found on this island: it is sandy, and a lot of pox-wood grows there. The Spaniards took cows and bulls over there to breed, but when the buccaneers came they destroyed everything.

West of San Domingo lies another handsome village called Azua. The people here trade with another village named San Juan de Goave, situated right in the middle of the island at the edge of a great prairie, at least twenty leagues in perimeter, full of wild cattle. No one lives in this village but cow-skinners or hunters. Most of them are of mixed blood – people of Negro and white parentage, known as mulattoes, or of Indian and white descent, called mestizos. Those of mixed Negro and Indian blood are nicknamed *alcatraces*. There is a great mingling of races, for the Spaniards are extremely fond of Negro women, more so than of their own. From this village comes a great quantity of hides and tallow, but nothing else is produced there on account of the great dryness of the soil.

The Spaniards possess all this island from Cabo de Lobos inland to San Juan de Goave to Cabo de Samana on the north side, and in the east from Punta de Espada to Cabo de Lobos. The rest of the island is occupied by French planters and forest hunters.

The island has some excellent harbours. Between Cabo de Lobos and Cabo de Tiburon in the west are four or five fine ports, far surpassing those of England. Around lie fair fields and valleys, and rivers of the purest water to be found in the whole world, with lovely beaches where the turtles come to lay their eggs. Two good havens lie between Cabo de Tiburon and Cabo Doña Maria; and from the latter to Cabo San Nicolas no less than twelve are found; while from there to Punta de Espada are twenty more. Every one is at the mouth of two or three confluent rivers, full of fish.

On the north side of the island there used to be various towns and villages, but these were destroyed by the Dutch, and the Spaniards have abandoned them.

CHAPTER FOUR

The fruits, trees and animals found on Hispaniola.

HISPANIOLA is extremely rich in all kinds of fruits. One finds vast fields, five or six leagues in perimeter, entirely covered with trees of sweet or bitter oranges. It is the same with lemon trees, although these do not thrive like those grown in Spain: the biggest lemons are no larger than a hen's egg, and they are more sour.

There are also great plains of palm trees, exceedingly tall and delightful to see. They grow some 150 to 200 feet tall without branches, and at the top is a bush which looks and tastes like white cabbage, from which the leaves and seed-vessels sprout. The seeds form once a year out of this bushy part – which is extremely good to eat boiled with meat, being as savoury as a garden cabbage; the seeds serve as food for the wild swine.

Each tree has no more than a dozen leaves, and every month a leaf falls off and another grows in its place. They are about three or four feet wide, and six or seven feet in length. They are as tough as can be, and are used for covering the houses, and for packing up smoked meat, which I shall describe later on. The stalks of these leaves are green on the outside and very white inside, and from the innermost part one can peel off a certain skin, about the thickness of parchment, on which you can write as on paper. In rainy weather, there is no need to get wet in the forest if you can obtain some of these leaves. They will also serve to fetch water to drink, in time of need, for you can make buckets of them which will hold water, although they will not last more than seven or eight days.

The trees are very hard, but the outer wood is no thicker than three or four inches: inside is a softer substance you can cut with a knife. The trunks are about twelve feet in girth, of a fairly even size all the way up. They grow on level ground, in salty soil. Wine can be made from these palms, in the following way. When the tree has been lopped off, about three or four feet from the root, a four-sided incision is made in the bushy part on top – from which in the course of time the wine comes gently dripping out, and is strong enough to make men drunk. The French call this tree the frank-palm.

As well as this variety, there are four other species: the latania palm, the needle palm, the wine palm, and the mountain or rosary palm. The latania does not grow as tall as the wine palm, but has roughly the same form, except that its leaves are fan-shaped, measuring seven or eight feet round and set about with spines six inches long. This tree produces its seeds like the variety described before, but they are bigger and thicker, and serve as food for the wild animals. The leaves are used for covering houses. This tree seldom grows in good ground, but in sandy and rocky places.

The needle palm is so called because, from the root right up to the leaves on top, it is full of thorns, three or four inches long. Some Indian tribes in the southern part of America use these thorns for tormenting and hurting their prisoners of war. They tie the prisoner to a tree, and take some of these thorns and wrap each one in a little wad of cotton dipped in palm oil. They stick these in the victim's flesh as close as the thorns on the tree, and then set fire to them. If the victim sings, he is esteemed a valiant soldier who considers his enemies too small to hurt him; but they think him a faint-hearted wretch if he laments and groans. I had this story from an Indian who had often treated his enemies in this manner, and it has also been seen by Christians living among these tribes.

But to continue our account. The needle palm does not differ in height from the latania, but its leaves are like those of the frank-palm, except that they have no stems. A good wine can be made from this palm too, as previously described. The seeds are produced as on the other palms, but they are rounder and bigger. Inside is a kernel which is very hard, and tastes as good as a walnut. The trees grow on low ground by the sea-shore.

The wine palm gets its name because it produces wine in great quantity. It grows no higher than forty or fifty feet, and is of an extraordinary shape. From the root up to about half its height or more, its girth is no bigger than three or four handspans – but from half or two-thirds up, it swells out as big as a hogshead. This thick part is full of a certain substance which is like the heart of a cabbage, but full of sap of a delicious taste, which when fermented is as strong as wine. The juice is pressed out after the tree has been chopped down, which is easily done, for it can be cut with a big knife called a machete, shaped like a pastry-cook's knife.

When the tree has been cut down, they make a square incision in the middle of the thick part, which is called the barrel. They pound the barrel until it becomes very soft, and then they press the sap out with their hands. The tree itself provides all the utensils needed, for they filter the juice through the leaves, and from the lowest leaves make vessels to hold the wine and to drink it from. This tree produces its seeds like the other palms, but they are of a different appearance. They are of the colour and size of cherries and are good to eat, but they cause a sore throat. The trees grow on high and rocky ground.

The *palmiste à chapelet* or rosary palm gets its name because the Spaniards use its small, very hard seeds as beads to tell their prayers on. The trees are very tall and slender, with few leaves, and grow on the high mountain-tops.

Also found on this island are big tall trees which bear fruit as large as an ordinary melon (such as is grown in Europe) with a kernel in the middle the size of a hen's egg. The flesh is the colour of a melon, but grey on the outside. It tastes like an apricot and in fact the French call it an *abricot*. The wild pigs get very fat on them, and the French hunters eat them instead of bread.

Then there are other trees like pear trees, called *caimitos*, which bear fruit the shape and colour of big black plums, full of milky juice and very sweet. Inside are five or sometimes three kernels, the size of runner beans. The wild swine eat these too, but they are not to be found everywhere.

There are also some large trees with a fruit called genipas. The tree grows as tall as the black cherry, and the leaves are similar, but the branches spread very wide. The fruit is shaped like a poppy-head, but is about the size of two fists. The skin is grey in colour, and inside it is full of little pips, each enclosed in a membrane. This pellicle is very bitter, and if the fruit is eaten without its being removed, it causes constipation and great pain in the bowels.

If you squeeze the juice out of an unripe fruit, it is as black as soot and you can write on paper with it – but after nine days it fades away completely, as if the paper had never been written on. The wood of this tree is used for building, as it is solid and handsome timber. It would be good for ship-building, for it lasts well in water.

There are many more fruit trees, which other authors have described, and many cedars, much sought after for building ships and making canoes. These canoes are made of a single hollowed trunk, without any fittings such as seats, and they can sail against the best boat or sloop in existence. The Indians make them without any iron tools. They burn off the tree close to the root, and know how to control the fire so it does not burn further than they wish. When the tree has been felled, they make a big fire on top of the trunk. Some stand around with water ready to quench the fire where needed, and others scrape out the burnt wood with stone axes, managing to shape the trunk in the proper fashion. In these canoes they can put to sea twenty, eighty, or even a hundred leagues.

Great quantities of pox-wood or *lignum sanctum* grow on the island, and many other medicinal trees and shrubs, such as aloes and cassia and China-root, and the tree from which *gummi elemi* is obtained. There are trees from which dyes are obtained, such as the three kinds of sandalwood, and trees which provide timber for building houses and ships.

A tree called the mapou grows to an enormous size, and

is used for making canoes, but it is not so good as cedar. It is very spongy and soon becomes waterlogged. Acoma wood is very heavy and is like the boxwood, which grows in Europe, in colour. It is very useful for building purposes, particularly for making sails for the sugar-mills, since it is very hard. Oak is another timber used for house building, but it would be very serviceable for making ships, as it is extremely durable in water and, what is more, is not attacked by marine worms, as other woods are.

Brasilete or brazil-wood is quite well known in Europe: it is known as fustic, and is much used for dyeing. It grows in great quantity in the south of the island, especially in two places called Jacmel and Jaquina, which have harbours capable of receiving large ships.

The *manzanillo* grows on the sea-shore, with its branches hanging over the water. Its fruit is as sweet as our rennet apples, but is highly poisonous. As soon as anyone has eaten it, he becomes burning hot and thirsty; he changes colour, goes mad, and then dies. What is more, the fish that eat these fruit are poisonous, too. The fruit has a milky sap like that which comes from the fig tree, and if anyone gets it on his skin, blisters form as if he'd been burnt, and cause intense pain. Once I happened to take a branch from this tree to fan away mosquitoes from my face. Next day, my face was all swollen and covered with blisters, and I was three days without being able to see.

Another tree which grows by the sea-shore has fruit like damsons, with a stone inside; there are two kinds, white and black. The wild swine come to the beach to eat these fruit when they are ripe, and grow very fat on them. These trees, which the Spaniards call *icacos*, grow on the shore and spread their branches over the sand. They grow no taller than the thickets on our dunes at home.

Having given a short description of the trees and fruits of Hispaniola, we shall say something of the insects and reptiles found there. Although there are no venomous creatures on the whole island, there are three sorts of gnat which plague people so much they can scarcely endure it, especially if they are newcomers.

The first kind are the size of the gnats we have on summer days at home; they land on one's flesh and suck blood until they are full and unable to fly. In places where they are abundant the only thing to do is to break off a branch and keep fanning it, as a cow waves her tail to chase the flies away. They torment people most in the mornings and evenings, and most vexing of all is the noise they make in one's ears, which is not to be borne. These gnats are called *mosquitoes* by the Spaniards, and *maranguines* by the French.

The second sort is no bigger than a grain of sand. They are more artful than the mosquitoes, for they make no noise, and are able to creep through one's linen. The hunters in the woods smear their faces with hog's lard to protect them from this nuisance, and in the evenings burn tobacco in their tents or they would get no rest. These insects are active in the mornings and evenings and throughout the night, but by day one is free of them if there is the slightest breeze, for the least touch of coolness sends them away.

The third sort is a red mosquito the size of a mustard seed. These do not sting, but take a bite out of the skin, which forms a scab. The face swells up so much a man is quite disfigured. They are active throughout the day, from sunrise to sunset, but all through the night one is free of them. The Spaniards call them *rojados*, and the French call them *calarodes*.

There is another creature the colour and shape of a glow-worm, only rather bigger and longer, with two little spots on its head which shine by night. When they are in clusters of three or four in a tree, anyone would think it was a fire. I have had three of them in a hut, and could easily read a book by the light they gave. I wanted to bring some of them back to Europe, but they died of the cold. The light goes out immediately they are dead, or if they are squeezed. The Spaniards call them *moscas de fuego*, or fire-flies. There are also many insects like crickets: when anyone passes close by them they will sing till they burst.

There are many kinds of reptiles, including snakes, but none of them venomous. They do damage among the fowls, pigeons and other birds, but otherwise are very useful for clearing a house of rats and mice. They are so cunning they will squeak like a rat to entice the others. They do not chew the flesh, but first suck the animal's blood and then swallow the body whole, and it stays inside the snake until it rots away.

There are other reptiles called fly-catchers, which live on the flies they catch and do harm to nothing else. Then there are the land tortoises, which are very good to eat, and live in pools and swampy places. When the tobacco crop is ready, vast numbers of caterpillars appear. Once they attack a field of tobacco, there is no getting rid of them. Sometimes people are forced to cut down all the tobacco and throw it away. These creatures grow as thick as a finger.

There are also some very hideous spiders, with a body as big as an egg; their legs are as thick as those of a small crab, and they are hairy all over. They have four black teeth, as large as a young rabbit's, and give a very nasty bite. Even so, they are not venomous. They live in the roofs of houses. In the reeds along the pools one finds millipedes or scolopendria, to give them their Latin name [*sic*] and also scorpions, but not of the poisonous kind. If a man is bitten by one of them, there is no need to apply an antidote. The wound swells at first, but afterwards heals on its own. Throughout the whole island, there are no creatures to harm men by their venom.

We must not omit to mention the cayman, a species of crocodile which abounds on this island and grows to an amazing length and bulk. Some have been found seventy feet long and twelve feet in girth. These reptiles exercise a remarkable cunning in getting their food. They lie floating in the rivers, like rotten logs drifting in the water. They keep close to the bank, and when a wild boar or a cow comes down to drink, they seize the animal, drag it down to the bottom and drown it. To give themselves more power for this purpose,

the caymans swallow a hundredweight or two of stones –
for they are so light that otherwise they would be unable to
stay on the bottom. When they have caught an animal, they
leave it three or four days before eating it, for they cannot
bite into it until it is half rotten.

When the cow-killers have left hides to dry on the grass
near a river, these creatures will come and slide the skins into
the water down to the bottom, where they pile stones on
them and leave them until the hair has rotted off – this I have
seen for myself. I shall set down a few more of the observations I have made on the cayman, for I doubt if any of the
authors who have written of these reptiles have ever had such
experience of them as I have.

A trustworthy person told me he had once gone down to a
river to wash his tent, when a cayman came towards him,
caught hold of the tent and began hauling it into the water.
Curious to see the outcome, the man let the tent be pulled to
the edge of the bank, preparing to go in after it himself if
need be, and taking a sharp knife in his mouth. Then he
tugged at the tent as hard as he could, but was unable to hold
it back, and the cayman dragged him with it down to the
bottom. Letting go of the tent, the cayman then attacked the
man, lashing out with its feet in order to drown him. The
river was clear, so the man could see everything the cayman
did, and when he could not bear to be under water any
longer. he stuck the knife in the creature's belly. The cayman
instantly left off the attack, and died of the wound. The man
dragged it out of the water, and found in its belly more than
a hundredweight of stones – all sorts of small stones about the
size of a fist.

These creatures cannot hide, for even when you cannot see
them you can smell them, as they give off a very strong odour
of musk. They have glands between the skin and the flesh
where the musky substance forms. There are two in the throat,
two below the forelegs and two between the hindlegs. The
hunters save these glands to send to Europe for sale.

The caymans hatch out of eggs. Once a year, about the

45

month of May, they lay the eggs on the sandy shore, scratch sand over them to cover them, then leave them to hatch out. They are about the size of goose eggs, with an uneven shell, prickly inside. They are as white as birds' eggs, and taste good.

When the eggs are hatched, the young ones come creeping out like little ducklings and make straight for the water, where they stay floating on the surface for the first nine days. To protect them from being pounced on by the birds, the mother can swallow them up. In the daytime, if the weather is fine, she will lie on the sand in the sun, and the young ones will crawl out and frolic round about – but if anyone approaches, back they creep again into the mother's body. This I have seen myself. A cayman was sunning herself on the far side of a river, and when I threw a stone, I saw all the young ones scuttle back into her belly.

These caymans generally go by the name of crocodiles.

CHAPTER FIVE

*The animals and birds of Hispaniola, and the
French hunters and planters of that island.*

HISPANIOLA is not only endowed with an abundance of
wild fruits, and a fertile soil suitable for all kinds of crops, but
also teems with animals – such as horses, wild boar and wild
cattle – which can feed the population and help to establish
the island's trade.

There are also huge numbers of wild dogs which ravage
the other creatures; no sooner has a cow or mare given birth
than the dogs will eat up her young, if no help is to hand.
They run in packs of fifty or sixty together, and dare take on
a troop of wild boar. They will not leave off the attack until
two or three of the prey have been bitten to death.

A hunter was once the cause of my seeing something so
amazing I'd have been unable to believe it if anyone else had
told me the tale. One day I had gone hunting with this man,
when we heard the noise of a pack of wild dogs harrying a
boar. We left our hounds in the charge of a bond-servant we
had with us, and each approached with gun on shoulder. When
we drew near the scene, we each climbed up a tree to watch.
The dogs had the boar at bay against a tree, and stood barking
all round yet dare not move in to finish him off. The wild boar
reared up on his hind legs against the tree, and if a dog rushed
at him and he managed to gore it with his tusks, that dog did
not come back a second time.

After they had held the boar at bay for about an hour, he
tried to escape, but one of the dogs sprang at him from behind
and tore off his balls at a single bite. Immediately all the rest
of the pack leapt on him and bit the boar to death. As soon
as the animal's movements ceased, the dogs drew back and
lay down, all except the hound which had found the prey in

47

the first place. Only when this hound had eaten its fill did the rest of the pack join in, and in less than half an hour the animal was devoured entirely. One might well say these beasts have a certain intelligence, teaching people to bestow honour where it is due, for these dogs gave precedence to the hound which had tracked down the wild boar.

The man who was with me had seen similar events on various occasions. In every pack of dogs there is one which goes out and seeks the prey. As soon as it finds a quarry, all it does is give five or six barks, and when the rest of the pack comes up, it looks on while they get to work. I have seen the same sort of thing among tame dogs. The hunters always have with them one hound to seek out prey, and once it has found, it lies quietly until the hunters have killed the beast. Then the hunter rewards it with a piece of meat, after which it runs off to quest for more. All the other dogs stay with the hunters until they hear the beagle give tongue.

Aware of the havoc they inflict among the wild life of the island, and the great trouble the hunters had in obtaining meat to supply the people on the plantations, M. Bertrand d'Ogeron, the governor of Tortuga, attempted to destroy the wild dogs once and for all. In 1668 he sent for poison from France, and when it arrived he had several horses shot and the carcasses cut up and strewn with the poison. Poisoned bait was spread about for six months –without any appreciable lessening in the numbers of wild dogs.

These animals can be tamed – a thing which often happens. The hunters come across a litter and take the pups and train them, when they can be used for hunting.

The reader may be curious to know how the wild dogs came on the island, and I will explain, so far as I know. When the Spaniards made themselves masters of Hispaniola, the island was full of Indians. These men, seeing the Spaniards wanted to overpower them under pretext of friendship, rebelled against the Spanish rule and did their conquerors so much damage the Spaniards felt compelled to destroy them. But the Indians had hidden themselves in the forest, and the Spaniards could think of no better method than to bring in dogs to track them down. When any were found, the Spaniards hacked them to pieces and fed them to the hounds.

Since that time, the Indians have been so terrified they dare not show themselves, and most of them have perished of hunger, having hidden themselves among the rocks out of fear. I myself have seen caves in the mountains full of human bones, which I would guess to be the bones of more than a hundred people; I have come across many such caves when hunting. When no more Indians were to be seen, the Spaniards let some of their dogs run loose, and it seems probable the wild dogs have bred from these, for they are not native to the country.

The horses of the island are small in stature, with a short body, a thick head, a long neck and sturdy legs – not handsome creatures, by any means. They run in herds of two or three hundred together. If anyone comes in sight, the leader of the herd gallops ahead until he is five or six hundred paces from the humans, then he gives a snort and turns, and the whole herd wheels round after him.

These horses are very easy to tame. The hunters catch them for carrying meat or hides down to the coast. They stretch a rope across narrow forest tracks along which the horses pass, and when a horse treads against it, the bent sapling to which the rope is tied springs up so that the animal is checked. Once caught, the horses are tied up and given a beating, and made to drag something around to break them in. By this means, in eight days the animals become quite tame, and as inured to carrying a load as a farm-horse that has never done anything else. Having trained them in this way, the hunters can let them loose.

There used to be huge numbers of wild bulls and cows, but nowadays they are beginning to become scarce, being rapaciously preyed on from every side. The Spaniards destroy as many as they can, to grieve the French; the wild dogs devour many of their calves; and the French hunters in their turn slaughter them in great quantity. These bulls are very strong, sturdy animals. They are fierce when provoked or tormented, but otherwise keep out of people's way. Their hides measure from eleven up to thirteen or fourteen feet in length.

It is a wonder there still remains a single bull or wild boar on Hispaniola. For the past eighty-one years, more than 1500 wild swine have been destroyed every day, both by the Spaniards and the French. Indeed, from my own experience, I would say the French alone slaughter more than this every day, yet despite all this destruction there is still an incredible quantity of wild pigs on the island. They are of medium size, and generally black, other colours seldom being seen. They run in herds of fifty to sixty; the males always take the lead, with the females and young ones in the rear. When attacked by dogs they all scatter and rush off as fast as they can. There are always some groups which wander on their own, and these are always the best animals.

The wild swine can be tamed, as I know from experience. We have caught piglets in the forest, and brought them up on meat. When they were grown up, they used to follow us like dogs. They would run ahead of us into the trees, and when they met with any wild swine, they would start grunting and squealing, and the hounds rushed up directly. When the wild boar had been killed, the tame pigs would eat the raw flesh like the hounds, and then they would follow us again.

There are birds of many kinds on Hispaniola, most of them edible. There are wood-fowl, parrots and wild pigeons, crab-eaters, herons, ravens and West Indian turkeys. There are flamingos, fishers, frigate-birds and noddies, snipe, ducks, geese, teal, humming-birds and many others whose names are unknown to me.

The Spaniards call the wood-fowl *pintados* on account of their plumage, which is very smartly painted in black and white like the skin of a tiger. They do not have a comb on their heads like other fowls, but a sort of horny crest. They are about as big as the largest of our hens at home, and their taste is similar. They run in the woods in flocks of about fifty or sixty, and the instant they become aware of anybody they fly up into the trees with a great squawking. The eggs are laid on the ground, and it is easy to find them. They can be hatched under an ordinary hen, but when the chicks begin to grow big and hear the noise of the others in the forest, at once they run off to the woods and become wild again.

Parrots are found in great numbers around the fields. They usually nest in old palm trees, in holes where other birds have previously made their nests, for the parrot has a curved bill incapable of pecking out a hole. Nature, it would seem, has made up for this deficiency by providing small birds called *carpinteros*, or woodpeckers, whose beaks can bore through the hardest trees, which would blunt the sharpest axe. These birds are roughly the size of a sparrow and have a beak about an inch and a half long, with such power in it that in a week they can make a hole to nest in.

Vast flocks of pigeons are found everywhere, but they are edible only at a certain season, as we mentioned before when writing about Tortuga. The pigeons here are bigger than those on Tortuga, and when the trees are in fruit they grow so fat that when you shoot them their crops burst as they fall.

Crab-eaters are birds the size of a heron, and live on the crabs they find in the pools – hence their name. They are good to eat, and have seven galls in seven places in the body. The herons are no different from those we have in Europe.

There are also multitudes of ravens, which live on carrion left by the wild dogs or thrown away by the hunters. When shooting is going on, they gather in such crowds and make such a screeching the hunters cannot hear one another speak. They look just like the ravens in Europe, and can be eaten in time of need.

The West Indian turkeys are big-bodied birds, the size of the turkeys we know at home, but with different head and feet and plumage. They have a beak and feet like a stork, and are completely white apart from two black patches on the wings.

The flamingos live in the southern parts of the island. They have a body like a stork's, with a neck nearly six feet long and legs in proportion. Their beak is like that of a goose, but thicker and more curved, with a tongue an inch thick. They are extremely delicious to eat. These birds fly in flocks of fifty or sixty. When they are on the shore seeking their food, one of them always keeps watch. If he sees any danger, he gives a warning cry and flies off, and the whole flock immediately follows.

The fishers live on the banks of rivers and eat nothing but fish. They are white birds, the size of a duck, with a curved red beak about nine inches long, and red feet.

The frigate-birds fly at great speed and so delicately it is impossible to discern any movement. They fly far out to sea and live only on fish. They are about the size of a turkey; their flesh tastes like beef and is very nourishing. No one has ever seen these birds on land. They make their nests in those trees which grow in the water, with as many branches in the water as above it.

When they have not caught enough fish to feed their young, they fly around the crags which certain other birds inhabit, and strike at these birds with their wings until they are forced to flee – and in order to be lighter for their flight, they spew up all they have caught that day. But the frigate-birds dart rapidly beneath them and catch the disgorged food before it can drop into the sea.

The other poor birds often have to go to sleep with nothing in their crops. They are called noddies, because they yield to birds less powerful than themselves – for their beaks are stronger than those of the frigate-birds. These noddies are about the size of ducks, with a beak like a heron's, and like a saw on both sides. They live on fish, and frequent the trees which grow in the water.

These birds will let themselves be taken by men without any resistance other than screeching. When ships sail by the islands, the noddies come and perch on the yards. The sailors often catch them, but they are not good to eat, having an oily smell and taste. A bird with a similar oily taste is known as the great-throat, for it can swallow a fish as big as a man's head, although the bird itself is no bigger than a goose. It has a beak about eight inches long and four wide. These birds always frequent river-banks, the sea-shore or rocky islets.

The snipe are similar to those we have at home, but somewhat bigger and fatter. Ducks are found in immense numbers, and are in season at a certain time of the year just as in our own country. But they are so fat you have to burn the grease off them before you can eat them, and the same is true of the teal.

Geese come here once a year, and stay some three or four months. They stuff themselves with certain seeds until they become too fat to fly, and can easily be caught as they waddle along – a thing I've often done. We used to come across a flock of geese in the open plains and follow them until they could neither fly nor walk, when we could kill them easily with a stick. After gorging like this, they stay for a month apparently without eating anything, but living only on their fat, until they become light enough to fly.

The humming-bird is the tiniest of all the birds on the face of the earth. It has plumage of extreme beauty, and lives merely on flowers. Only the Indians are swift enough to shoot these small creatures with their arrows; they dry them and sell them to the Christians. When wishing to shoot these little birds, they put a drop of wax on the tip of their arrows and aim with great skill, so that the bird is undamaged.

It now remains for us to speak of the French on Hispaniola. I have already told how they came to the island, bringing their bond-servants with them and holding them in service for three years. Now I shall describe their customs and their manner of life and work.

The French on Hispaniola have three sorts of employment – hunting, planting and privateering. When a man has finished his service, he seeks out a partner and they pool all they possess. They draw up a document, in some cases saying that the partner who lives longer shall have everything, in others that the survivor is bound to give part to the dead man's friends or to his wife, if he was married. Having made this arrangement, some go off marauding, others to hunt, and others to plant tobacco, as they think best.

There are two sorts of hunters: those who hunt bulls for the hides, and those who go after wild boar, to sell the meat to the planters. The hunters of bulls became known as *boucaniers*. Formerly there used to be a good five or six hundred of them on the island, but now they are less than three hundred strong; the cattle have become so scarce the hunters have to be very quick and skilful to catch any.

The men stay a whole year, sometimes even two years, without leaving the woods, and then cross over to Tortuga to fetch necessaries – powder and shot, muskets, linen and so forth. When they arrive, they squander in a month all the money which has taken them a year or eighteen months to earn. They drink brandy like water, and will buy a whole cask of wine, broach it, and drink until there's not a drop left. Day and night they roam the town, keeping the feast of Bacchus so long as they can get drink for money. The service of Venus is not forgotten, either. In fact, the tavern-keepers and whores make ready for the coming of the hunters and the privateers in the same way as their fellows in Amsterdam prepare for the arrival of the East India ships and men-of-war. Once their money is all spent and they've had all they can on credit, back they go to the woods again, where they remain for another year or eighteen months.

Now we shall describe the sort of life they lead there. Having met at the rendezvous, they separate into troops of five or six hunters, with their indentured servants if they have any. Each band seeks a well situated place near the open fields, where they set up their tents and make a hut in which to store the hides when dry.

In the morning, as soon as it begins to get light, the hunters call up their hounds and go into the forest, along the trails where they hope to meet most bulls. Immediately they have shot a beast, they take what they call their brandy – that is, they suck all the marrow from the bones before it is cold. After this, they flay the beast properly, and one of them takes the hide to their rendezvous. They carry on like this until every man has got a hide; this takes until about noon – sometimes later, sometimes sooner. When they are all met together at the rendezvous, if they have bond-servants, these have to stretch out the hides to dry, and prepare the food. This is always meat, for they eat nothing else.

Having eaten, every man takes his gun and they go off to shoot horses for sport, or to bring down birds with a single bullet. Or they may shoot at targets for a prize – usually at an orange tree, to see who can shoot off most oranges without damaging them, but only nicking the stem with a single bullet – which I've often seen done.

Sundays they spend carrying the hides down to the beach and putting them in the boats. There was once a bondsman who badly wanted to have a rest, and told his master God had ordained seven days in a week –six for labour and the seventh for rest. His master did not interpret matters this way. He thrashed the lad unmercifully with a stick, saying 'Get on, you bugger; my commands are these – six days shalt thou collect hides, and the seventh shalt thou bring them to the beach.'

These men are cruel and merciless to their bondsmen: there is more comfort in three years on a galley than one in the service of a *boucanier*. There was one hunter who knocked about his servant so violently he thought he had killed him, but when he had gone away, the lad got to his feet and staggered after his master, but could find neither him nor the meeting-place. He had no choice but to stay in the forest, without any weapon with which to get food. He had not even a knife – nothing except a hound which had stayed at his side.

After two or three days without food, he chanced upon a herd of wild swine, and the hound managed to catch one of the young ones. The lad had no means of making a fire to roast the pig; what is more, he had nothing with which to cut it open. Finally he succeeded in hacking it up with a piece of flint, and ate the flesh, raw as it was. He gave a lump to the hound, and kept the rest as long as he could, not knowing when he would find anything else, wandering all alone in the forest.

Once, while out hunting with his hound, he saw a wild bitch with a piece of meat in her mouth that she was carrying home to her whelps. He followed her until she came to her den, and began hurling stones in the nest until at last the wild bitch was stoned to death. Then he seized the meat she had been carrying and devoured it. He took two of the pups along with him, for as it happened his own hound was also a bitch which had recently had a litter, and still had enough milk to suckle these whelps.

Eventually, he found a place in the forest where he could catch enough young pigs to feed himself and his dogs. He became so accustomed to this life he stayed there a long time, hoping that some day the hunters would pass that way. He dared not go far from the place, being afraid he would be unable to find his way back, and then might have to go hungry again. As it was, his dogs soon grew big enough to hunt, so he was no longer short of food. He became used to eating raw flesh, and desired no other sort. His greatest lack was having no knife with which to cut the meat. When his dogs made a kill, he had first to wait until they had eaten and opened up the beast. Then he tore off lumps of flesh with his hands, and ate it with as much relish as the best food he had ever eaten in his life.

This existence went on for about fourteen months, when by chance he came across a band of hunters. They were scared when first they caught sight of him, for he looked utterly wild. In all that time he had not shaved, and he was completely naked apart from a strip of tree-bark which covered his loins, and he had a piece of raw flesh dangling at his side.

He told them how he had parted from his master. The hunters wanted to take him along with them, but he said they must release him from his bondage: he was resolved to continue living as he had the past year or more, rather than return to his master. They promised to do so, and brought him back

with them and advanced him enough money to buy his freedom.

I happened to be at the place when they brought him back,
and stared at him with amazement, for he was fat and sleek
and far healthier than when he had depended on his master.
He was so used to raw flesh he would not willingly eat cooked
meat, nor could his digestion tolerate it. As soon as he had
eaten any, he would be groaning the next hour or so with
stomach-ache, and would spew the meat up again as whole as
when he'd eaten it. But when he ate raw meat, all went well.
We tried to keep raw flesh from him as much as we could, but
he managed to get at it when we weren't looking.

I have noticed the same thing with wild dogs: after they
are a month or two old, they don't fancy cooked meat. I have
told this story to show the cruelty of these hunters to their
indentured servants, and also to show how a man can accus-
tom himself to all kinds of food. In fact, I believe a man could
live on grass just as well as animals do, and I shall bring up
further examples on this subject elsewhere.

The Spaniards keep the foreign hunters under constant
observation, and sometimes murder them if they get the
chance. Five companies of Spaniards have been sent out from
San Domingo to seek out the enemy – but praying they won't
find them. They have not the courage to meet them in the
open field, but try to spy out their whereabouts and do away
with them in their sleep.

I will briefly recount a few incidents on this subject. One
morning, a hunter was out with his servant, and twelve
Spaniards on horseback were concealed along the trail. He
noticed the prints of horses' hooves so took another way, yet
still could not give them the slip. They heard the barking of
his dogs, and rode down on him in an open field. Seeing there
was no escape, the hunter held his ground, setting powder and
bullets in his hat at his feet. The servant stood back to back
with him and did the same, and in this posture they awaited
the onslaught.

The twelve Spanish horsemen ringed them round, their

lances at the ready, calling on them to surrender and promising them mercy. The hunter put no trust in this promise: he had played too many tricks on the Spaniards before, and knew if they got hold of him they would burn him alive. He wanted no quarter, he told them, but the first one who attacked him should pay dearly for it. With this, he dropped on one knee and aimed his musket ready to fire. Seeing his determination, the Spaniards rode away and let him go.

On another occasion, a hunter out on his own was surprised by a troop of Spaniards. He began to run towards them, calling out as if he had more men at his back, and aiming his musket. Terrified, the Spaniards fled, letting him get off scot-free.

The other hunters hunt nothing but wild boar, salting the meat and selling it to the planters. There is no difference between their manner of life and that of the hunters of cattle. But their method of catching the wild boar is very different from the way they hunt in Europe.

These men have regular sites where they stay for three or four months, or sometimes even a year. They call such places *boucan*. Usually five or six men go off together. A hunter will make an agreement with a planter to provide his house with meat for a twelvemonth, getting in return twenty or thirty hundredweight of tobacco. Moreover, he is given a bond-servant to assist him, whom the planter is obliged to keep in powder, shot and hounds. All the rest of his needs the hunter must supply for himself.

The hunters have a few extra perquisites, however. When they have done their morning's work, they go off in the afternoons to shoot horses, and melt the fat to make lamp-oil. They sell this tallow to the planters for a hundredweight of tobacco the pot. They earn still more if they rear hounds for sale, as a good hunting-dog will fetch six pieces of eight, which is the set price.

Other hunters, not bound by any such agreement, go off in groups of seven or eight, one man carrying all the guns and another leading the hounds. One of the party stays on his own at the *boucan*, to look after the goods, smoke the flesh, grind salt and do the cooking against the return of the rest of the party. They kill great numbers of animals, sometimes shooting a hundred wild swine in a morning – only to take seven or eight of them, because in general they prefer to have sows. These are always fatter than the boars, apart from those hogs which go off and seek food on their own. These animals can do great damage to men and dogs if they are not careful. A man must always carry a staff, to fend off the boar if it is only wounded. Once the wounded boar has gone by, there is no more danger, for these animals never turn in their tracks, but always charge straight ahead.

When the hunting party has returned, each man flays the animals he has caught and removes the flesh from the bones. The meat is cut into strips about six feet long, sometimes more, sometimes less. The cut meat is strewn with ground salt and left in salt three or four hours. Then it is hung on sticks and beams in a hut near by. They light a fire under it and smoke the meat until it is sufficiently dry and hard, then pack it away. When they have accumulated twenty or thirty hundredweight they take it along to sell to the planters, receiving two pounds of tobacco for every pound of meat.

Having described the life of the hunters, we will now consider the planters. They began cultivation on Tortuga about the year 1598, and the first crop they planted was tobacco. This did very well, but they were unable to make many plantations as the island is so small, with little agricultural land. They also wanted to plant sugar, but this made no progress, for there was no one to put up the money needed for a sugar refinery.

Consequently, as I said, most folk took to hunting or privateering, but when hunting grew slack on the island, some of them turned to agriculture again, choosing the best place they could find for planting tobacco in the whole of Hispaniola. The first places they settled were in Cul de Sac, in the north-west of the island, and in time their numbers grew, so that now they are a good two thousand strong. They are safe from the Spaniards, who cannot get at them.

At first they suffered great hardship while preparing the ground, for while occupied with this task they could not be out seeking food. Where now they have their plantations, in those days it was all forest, full of wild boar. To begin with, they had no other means of support. When they started to cultivate, they divided the land into separate sections, beginning their planting in a small way. Two or three would join together and buy the necessary tools, such as axes, mattocks and knives, with five or six hundredweight of provisions, and beans for the first food-crop. Then they would go off into the forest, and build themselves a hut of branches, where they lived until things improved.

The first job was to clear the undergrowth, which they laid in small piles to dry. Then they cut down the tall trees and stripped off the branches, which they burnt with the dry brushwood, keeping the trunks. The first crop they sowed was beans, which are ripe and dry in six weeks. Then they put in sweet potatoes and manioc, and afterwards the corn which is their staple food. The sweet potatoes take four or five months to ripen, but the manioc needs eight or nine months or sometimes a whole year before it is good to eat. When ripe, it can be left in the ground another twelve-month, but after that it goes bad, so it must be used within the year.

These three crops provide their food. They cook the beans with meat, and make a pottage of them with eggs. They have sweet potatoes in the morning for breakfast: they are cooked in a big pan with a little water, covered closely with a cloth, and in half an hour they are ready and as dry as chestnuts. They are served with butter and a sauce made of lemon juice, lard and red peppers. Some of these cooked sweet potatoes are put aside to make a drink. The planters cut them in slices in a crock and pour on hot water. The liquor is strained through a cloth into a cauldron, and after standing two or three days it begins to ferment. It makes a very good and nourishing drink, with a sour taste which is not unpleasant. They call it *maby*, a name learnt from the Indians.

The manioc, or cassava, serves as bread, and is prepared in this manner. They scrape the manioc roots with graters of copper or tin, as they do horse-radish in Holland. When they have grated as much as they need, they put the shavings in sacks of coarse cloth and press all the moisture out until it is perfectly dry, and then pass it through a large parchment sieve. After sifting, it looks just like sawdust. They bake it on a hot iron griddle into a sort of cake, and then put these on the roof-tops to dry in the sun. Perhaps this is where the old story comes from, of the land where the houses were covered with pancakes.

So as not to waste any, they use the coarse meal that will not pass through the sieve to make cakes five or six inches thick, which they pile on top of each other and leave to ferment. This produces a liquor like beer, which tastes very good and is most nourishing. There are various other fruits, such as bananas, which they cook with meat, and also make into a liquor by adding water, as with sweet potatoes. The drink made from bananas is as strong as wine and, if you take too much, makes you drunk and gives you a severe headache.

When the plantations were producing food-crops, the men began clearing and cultivating the ground ready to plant tobacco. They sow the tobacco seeds in beds about twelve feet square, fenced round and covered closely with palm leaves to keep out the sun. The beds are watered every evening, if it has not rained. When the tobacco is as big as lettuce, it is transplanted into rows three feet apart, with each plant three feet from the next. The most suitable time for planting is from January to the end of March, which is the rainy time of the year. The ground must be kept well weeded. When the to-bacco is about eighteen inches high and grown into a thick bush, the tips are snipped off to prevent it growing taller, so that the leaves get all the nourishment and become thick and vigorous.

While the tobacco is growing, they make the drying-sheds.

These are fifty to sixty feet long and thirty or forty feet wide, fitted with poles lying across the beams from top to bottom, on which to spread the tobacco. When the plants are fully grown they are cut and put to dry in these sheds. Then the leaves are stripped from the stalks and rolled up by special workers who do nothing else, and receive a tenth of what they roll, as wages. The plants sprout more leaves after they have been cut, and this happens four times a year. The produce is exported to France and other countries, and is mostly used for chewing-tobacco and for dye.

The French planters on Hispaniola have always been subjects of the governor of Tortuga, as they still are today, yet not without resistance on their part. The colony set up by the French West India Company on Tortuga in 1664 included the planters on Hispaniola. These men strongly resented the attempt to bring them under subjection, in a land which belonged neither to the King nor the Company, and resolved not to work rather than be dominated. Deriving nothing but loss from the enterprise, the Company promptly closed it down.

The governor* of Tortuga, who was quite popular with the planters, thought he could find a better means to control them. He announced that he had all kinds of goods they needed, and would make a much better bargain with them than any foreign traders. Since he was favourably disposed towards them, he would arrange for ships to carry their merchandise to France four times a year and bring back things they required. This would be much better than selling their goods to foreigners.

He managed to get the most important planters on his side, and excluded the rest from all benefits. They could not buy so much as a yard of linen without begging and praying, and they could not export their produce. The ships that called in were under his orders, and he himself was one of the

---

* *Translator's note:* In 1667, de Pouancey replaced his uncle, d'Ogeron, as governor. He was called Gouverneur de Saint-Domingue, not of Tortuga.

ship-owners. His own goods were loaded first, and then the merchandise of his friends, and if there was still any room on board, only those with the governor's permission were given the necessary papers.

In 1669, while all this was going on, the planters had news of two Dutch ships lying off the coast of Hispaniola. They made up their minds to defy the governor and trade with these ships. Shortly afterwards the governor arrived, but they would not let him land, shooting at him so that he dare not come ashore. He was compelled to turn back to Tortuga, and send his ships to France half laden.

Meanwhile, the Dutch ships entered harbour. The friends and officials of the governor would have liked to have forbidden the trade, but had to keep quiet or they'd have had their necks broken. The trade with the Dutch proceeded, and both ships sailed out with a full cargo of hides and tobacco, promising to return for more. Without a doubt they would have done so, if the war had not prevented it.

The planters were so bitterly hostile to the governor that they got together a raiding-party, a man from every house, and crossed to Tortuga in canoes, bent on capturing the island and putting the governor to death. They were confident they could always count on the assistance of the Dutch to supply all their needs – and I certainly believe this would have been the case, but for the war.

While this was going on, the governor had sent a messenger to France asking help from the King, implying that these troublemakers were capable of seizing all his islands. The result of this cunningly worded message was that he received two warships from the King to protect Tortuga.

The two men-of-war were sent to Hispaniola to bring the rebels back to obedience. Far from showing submission, once they saw the warships coming, every man took to the forest. The landing-parties set fire to their abandoned houses. The governor, however, sent them messages in a tone of clemency. The planters, realizing they could expect no one to come to their relief, promised obedience under certain conditions.

Nevertheless the governor had one or two of the ringleaders hanged, though he pardoned the rest and gave them permission to trade with whom they liked.

The plantations were again put in order and were soon yielding huge crops of fine tobacco. Altogether, they supply a good twenty-five to thirty thousand rolls of tobacco a year.

The planters have few slaves; mostly they do the work themselves, along with indentured servants bound to them for three years. They trade in human beings just like the Turks, selling bondsmen among themselves as people in Europe deal in horses. Some of them make it their business to go to France looking for labourers in the country towns and among the peasants. They make big promises, but when the lads get to the island they are sold and have to work like horses, harder in fact than the Negroes. For the planters admit they must take greater care of a Negro slave than a white bondsman, because the Negro is in their service for life, while the white man is theirs only for a period.

They treat their bond-servants as cruelly as the hunters do, showing them no pity at all. Whether sick or well, they must work all the same in the heat of the sun, which is sometimes intolerable. The backs of these wretched lads are often full of scabs of sunburn sores, like horses chafed by heavy loads.

The bondsmen are subject to a certain sickness, brought about by the change of air and the bad food. They become sleepy, dropsical and short of breath. This illness is known as *mal d'estomac*, and is caused only by the bad diet and the melancholy induced by the harsh treatment they suffer. Many of the youths have been lured away from good homes by these traders in living souls, and when they encounter such wretchedness they promptly fall ill of the endemic disease. Nevertheless, they are neither spared nor assisted. On the contrary, they are forced to work with blows, often until they drop down dead. Then the planters complain, 'The rascal would rather die than work.' I have often seen such cases, to my great sorrow. I will give a few examples.

A certain young man of good family came to the island on

account of the ill-treatment of his uncle, who was his guardian. He fell into the hands of one of these planters, who used him with extreme cruelty, wanting him to tackle work he could not possibly manage, and what is more giving him nothing to eat. He became so desperate he ran off into the forest, where he starved to death. I myself found his body, half eaten by the dogs.

No less memorable is the case of the planter whose bondsman ran off to the woods through ill-treatment, but was fetched back again. His master tied him to a tree, beat him till the blood gushed down his back, then smeared his flesh with a sauce made of lemon juice, salt and red pepper. He was left in this state, tied to the tree, for twenty-four hours. Then the master came back and struck him again, until he died under the blows. The last words the lad spoke were these: 'God grant the devil may torment you as long before your death as you have tortured me before mine.'

And three or four days after the youth's death, this tyrant – for I can call him nothing else – became plagued by an evil spirit, which tormented him night and day, nor ceased tormenting him so long as he was alive. He became covered with bruises and lacerations, so that he did not look like a man at all. I believe this came to pass by God's righteous judgement, to punish the criminal for all the murders he had committed under similar circumstances.

I knew three other lads who in desperation murdered their master, who had made them work night and day with nothing to eat, so that they were driven to beg a bit of cassava from their neighbours. These youths were hanged, and before they died testified that their master had also beaten one of their mates to death.

Atrocious cruelties of this kind were mostly committed by planters from the Caribbean islands, where they treat their bondsmen even more unmercifully than those on Hispaniola. There is one planter on St Kitts, Belteste by name, who has beaten to death more than a hundred lads. To make out he had treated them well, he used to have fresh meat and eggs and wine set out beside their corpses, so people would say he had taken good care of his servants. This man dared to say it made no difference to him whether he should be damned or saved, so long as he could leave enough wealth behind him for his children to have a coach and horses. The Dutch merchants who used to trade there knew this fellow well. I could say more on the subject, but the reader may judge the whole work from these samples.

The English treat their servants no better, but with greater cunning. The lads are usually indentured for seven years, and when they have served for six they are ill-treated beyond endurance, so that they are driven to beg their master to sell them to someone else. This request is not refused, which means they are sold for another seven years, or for three at the least. I have seen men who have been enslaved in this manner for fifteen, twenty and twenty-eight years. Often these fellows are so simple they will sell themselves for a whole year for the sake of a good meal.

The English celebrate Christmas with a great deal of eating and drinking, and at that season the masters let the slaves have whatever they ask for – yet they have to pay dearly for it in the end. The English have a strict law that when anyone owes the sum of twenty-five shillings and cannot pay up, he may be sold as a slave for a certain period, such as a year or six months.

Now I will delay the reader no longer, but come to our main purpose, which is to tell of the buccaneers.

CHAPTER SIX

The First Buccaneers.

I HAVE previously told how I was driven to join the pirates –
for I don't know what other name they deserve, as they were
not backed by any prince. This is evident from the various
occasions when the King of Spain sent his ambassadors to
complain of the activities of these people to the French and
English courts. No war was going on, yet this did not prevent
their capturing Spaniards and plundering their towns and
villages. The ambassadors were informed that these men were
not subjects of the French and English kings, and that His
Catholic Majesty could do what he would with them if they
fell into his hands. The King of France excused himself by
saying he had no fortifications on Hispaniola, and received no
tribute from the island. The King of England declared he had
never commissioned those on Jamaica to conduct hostilities
against His Catholic Majesty, and to satisfy the Spanish court
he recalled the governor of Jamaica and installed another in his
place. Meanwhile, the rovers continued their marauding.

The first buccaneer on Tortuga was a certain Pierre le
Grand of Dieppe, who, in the year 1602, with one boat and a
crew of twenty-eight, captured the vice-admiral of the Spanish
fleet off Cape Tiburon, in the west of Hispaniola. This was in
the days when the Spaniards had still not discovered the
Channel of Bahama, and went to sea by way of the Caicos.

According to the journal of a reliable person, this was how
the ship was taken. The buccaneer had been at sea a considerable time, without encountering any prey. Food was short,
and his vessel was in such bad shape as to be hardly seaworthy.
He then caught sight of this ship, which had strayed from the
rest of the fleet, and steered towards her, to find out what she
was. When they were so close she could not escape, le Grand

resolved to board her, judging the flagship would be unprepared for an attack. The crew agreed to obey their chief, saying the Spanish ship had no better chance than they to succeed in the encounter. They all swore an oath of loyal endeavour. Le Grand ordered the surgeon to bore a hole in the bottom of his barque, and they prepared to board the enemy.

It was nearly dark when they came alongside. Noiselessly they clambered on deck, with no other weapons than a pistol and a cutlass each. They encountered no resistance, and made for the cabin, where the captain and some others were playing cards. Instantly a pistol was clapped to his breast, and he was compelled to surrender the ship. Meanwhile, others had gone to the gun room and seized the arms. Some Spaniards who tried to prevent them were shot dead.

That very day the captain had been warned that the vessel on the horizon was a pirate and might do them harm. Contemptuously the captain had replied he would not fear a vessel that was his equal, much less a small boat such as that – yet, through his negligence, his ship was ignominiously captured.

The buccaneers' boat had already sunk to leeward of the flagship. Some of the Spaniards, seeing such strange folk on board their vessel, assumed they must have fallen from the sky. '*Jesus, son demonios estos!*' they cried. Le Grand kept as many of the Spanish sailors as he needed to run the ship and set the rest on shore. While still at sea, he sent for his commission, in order to be able to enter a port. Then he set sail for France in his capture, where he remained and never went to sea again.

On learning of the rovers' success, the planters and hunters of Tortuga forsook their plantations and hunting-grounds and looked out for means of acquiring ships in which to go and plunder the Spaniards. They set forth in their canoes towards Cape Alvarez in the north of Hispaniola, where they might intercept the barques which the Spaniards use for trading from one town to another along the coast, and for carrying hides and tobacco to Havana. The large Spanish ships travel no farther than the capital of Cuba.

The buccaneers captured several of these boats, laden with hides and tobacco, and brought them to Tortuga. Here they sold their plunder to merchant ships at anchor in the road-stead, and with the money bought necessaries such as powder, bullets and other useful arms. Then they prepared their barques for a fresh expedition towards the Gulf of Campeche and the Gulf of New Spain, where the Spaniards did a great deal of trading and had many ships. The buccaneers were not long without booty. Within a month they were back in Tortuga with two ships which had been bound for the coast of Caracas with a cargo of silver.

It was not long before they put to sea again in these two ships, and within a couple of years had a force of at least twenty vessels in quest of plunder. The Spaniards were compelled to equip several frigates to protect their shipping and cruise against the buccaneers.

CHAPTER SEVEN

*How the buccaneers equip their vessels, and their
manner of living.*

THE rovers can fit out an expedition cheaply, and easily come
by new vessels, in the way I have described. When a buccaneer
is going to sea he sends word to all who wish to sail with him.
When all are ready, they go on board, each bringing what he
needs in the way of weapons, powder and shot.

On the ship, they first discuss where to go and get food
supplies. This means meat – for they eat nothing else on their
voyages, unless they capture other foodstuffs from the Spaniards. The meat is either pork or turtle, which is also salted.
Sometimes they go and plunder the Spaniards' *corrales*, which
are pens where they keep perhaps a thousand head of tame
hogs. The rovers go at night and find the house of the farmer
who looks after the pigs and fetch him out of his bed. Unless
he gives them as many hogs as they demand, they hang him
without mercy.

When the rovers have to do their own hunting, they employ
a hunter of their own nationality who has a pack of hounds,
letting him have whatever share of the catch they think fit.
Some of them go with the hunter to help salt and smoke the
flesh, while others stay on board to get the vessel shipshape –
careening and greasing and doing all that is necessary. When
the hunting party have salted as much meat as they think will
suffice for the voyage, they bring it to the ship, where it is
piled in the hold on the ballast.

They cook two meals a day of this meat, without rationing.
When it is boiled, the fat is skimmed off the cauldron and put
into little calabashes, for dipping the meat in. The meal consists of only one course, and often it tastes better than the food
to be found on a gentleman's table. The captain is allowed

no better fare than the meanest on board. If they notice he has better food, the men bring the dish from their own mess and exchange it for the captain's.

When the provisions are on board and the ship is ready to sail, the buccaneers resolve by common vote where they shall cruise. They also draw up an agreement or *chasse partie*, in which is specified what the captain shall have for himself and for the use of his vessel. Usually they agree on the following terms. Providing they capture a prize, first of all these amounts would be deducted from the whole capital. The hunter's pay would generally be 200 pieces of eight. The carpenter, for his work in repairing and fitting out the ship, would be paid 100 or 150 pieces of eight. The surgeon would receive 200 or 250 for his medical supplies, according to the size of the ship.

Then came the agreed awards for the wounded, who might have lost a limb or suffered other injuries. They would be compensated as follows: for the loss of a right arm, 600 pieces of eight or six slaves; for a left arm, 500 pieces of eight or five slaves. The loss of a right leg also brought 500 pieces of eight or five slaves in compensation; a left leg, 400 or four slaves; an eye, 100 or one slave, and the same award was made for the loss of a finger. If a man lost the use of an arm, he would get as much as if it had been cut off, and a severe internal injury which meant the victim had to have a pipe inserted in his body would earn 500 pieces of eight or five slaves in recompense.

These amounts having first been withdrawn from the capital, the rest of the prize would be divided into as many portions as men on the ship. The captain draws four or five men's portions for the use of his ship, perhaps even more, and two portions for himself. The rest of the men share uniformly, and the boys get half a man's share.

When a ship has been captured, the men decide whether the captain should keep it or not: if the prize is better than their own vessel, they take it and set fire to the other. When a ship is robbed, nobody must plunder and keep his loot to himself. Everything taken – money, jewels, precious stones and goods – must be shared among them all, without any man enjoying a penny more than his fair share. To prevent deceit, before the booty is distributed everyone has to swear an oath on the Bible that he has not kept for himself so much as the value of a sixpence, whether in silk, linen, wool, gold, silver, jewels, clothes or shot, from all the capture. And should any man be found to have made a false oath, he would be banished from the rovers, and never more be allowed in their company.

The buccaneers are extremely loyal and ready to help one another. If a man has nothing, the others let him have what he needs on credit until such time as he can pay them back. They also see justice done among themselves. If anyone has a quarrel and kills his opponent treacherously, he is set against a tree and shot dead by the one whom he chooses. But if he has killed his opponent like an honourable man – that is, giving him time to load his musket, and not shooting him in the back – his comrades let him go free. The duel is their way of settling disputes.

When they have captured a ship, the buccaneers set the prisoners on shore as soon as possible, apart from two or three whom they keep to do the cooking and other work they themselves do not care for, releasing these men after two or three years.

The rovers frequently put in for fresh supplies at some island or other, often one of those islets lying off the south coast of Cuba. Here they drag the ship up the beach to careen her. Everyone goes ashore and sets up his tent, and they take turns to go on marauding expeditions in their canoes. They take prisoner the turtle-fishers of Bayamo – poor men who catch and sell turtles for a living, to provide for their wives and children. Once captured, these men have to catch turtle for the rovers as long as they remain on the island. Should the rovers intend to cruise along a coast where turtles abound, they take the fishermen along with them. The poor fellows may be compelled to stay away from their wives and families four or five years, with no news whether they are alive or dead.

Having mentioned turtles, which may be quite unfamiliar to many readers, I shall briefly describe them. In America there are four kinds of marine turtle. One species is immensely big, weighing up to three or four thousand pounds. These reptiles have no hard shell, so their flesh may easily be pierced with a knife, but they are full of oil and not fit to eat. The second sort are the green turtles; they are of middling size, being a good four feet in breadth. Their shell is thicker, covered with small scales about as thick as the horn used in lanterns. These turtles are extremely good to eat – the flesh very sweet and the fat green and delicious. This fat is so penetrating that when you have eaten nothing but turtle flesh for three or four weeks, your shirt becomes so greasy from sweat you can squeeze the oil out and your limbs are weighed down with it. The third kind is of similar size but with a bigger head, and is not fit to eat, for it reeks of oil. The fourth variety, known as caret, is smaller and longer in the body, and has a shell like those we know in Europe.

These turtles live among rocks under the water, feeding on the moss and sea-apples found there. The other varieties live on grass which grows under water: there are some banks as green and lush as the meadows in Holland. Here the turtles come at night to feed. They cannot stay long on the bottom without coming up to take breath; as soon as they have blown, they descend once more.

They lay eggs like the crocodiles, but without a shell, being covered only with a thin membrane like the skin inside a hen's egg. They produce such prodigious quantities of eggs that, if many were not destroyed by the birds, people could scarcely sail a boat in these parts without running into turtles. They lay three times a year, in May, June and July – and every time each turtle lays 150 or even 190 eggs. They come ashore, scratch out a hole in the sand to lay their eggs in, then cover them over again. The heat of the sun hatches the eggs in three weeks, and out come the young turtles and make for the sea. No sooner are they in the water than the gulls swoop down and snap them up, for they cannot submerge until nine days after their birth. It is lucky if two or three survive out of a hundred.

The turtles have particular places where they come every year to lay their eggs, their main haunt being the Cayman Islands. These are three in number, one big and two small, lying at 20° 15' north, some forty-five leagues south of Cuba. The turtles come to these islands in such immense numbers that every year a good twenty ships, English as well as French, take on a cargo of turtle flesh, which they salt. The males come to these places to mate with the females, and when two turtles copulate, they remain one or two whole days upon one another.

It is incomprehensible how these creatures manage to find the islands, having quitted other regions to get there; they come from the Gulf of Honduras, some 150 leagues away. Sometimes, ships which have missed their landfall through adverse currents and have been unable to find their latitude have finally set course by the noise of turtles blowing, and so reached the islands.

No special implements are carried for catching the green turtles (the only kind good to eat) but when these creatures come on shore every night to lay their eggs, they can be levered over by two men with a hand-spike. Once laid on their backs, the turtles cannot budge. When many ships lie waiting to load, the beach is divided so that the men from each ship have a certain stretch of sand to clear. In the length of 500 paces as many as a hundred turtles may be turned upside down.

When their season is over on the Cayman Islands, the turtles make for Cuba, where the sea-bed is clean, and here they eat – for all the time they are on the Caymans they eat nothing. Similarly, when a turtle has been caught it can stay about a month lying on its back and remain alive, but by then its fat will have changed to slime, and its flesh be tasteless.

When the turtles have been in Cuban waters a month or so and grown fat again, along come the Spanish fishers, such as those poor men the rovers capture and keep in slavery, to catch them and so provide food for their towns and villages. They fix a four-sided nail, about two inches long and barbed like a harpoon, to a long pole. When the turtle comes up to blow, they hurl this spear so that the dart sticks in its body. Then they pay out some fifteen or sixteen fathoms of line, and when the turtle comes up again to take breath, they throw another harpoon into its side, and so are able to haul the creature into the canoe. Sometimes they are shot on the sea-bed in four fathoms of water, the darker the better, for in the dark of night as the turtle swims its four feet give off a flickering light and its shield looks quite white, so it can easily be seen. These creatures have very keen sight but cannot hear, so far as one can tell.

The buccaneers' main exercises are target-shooting and keeping their guns clean. They use good weapons, such as muskets and pistols. Their muskets are about four and a half feet long, and fire a bullet of sixteen to a pound of lead. They use cartridges, and have a cartouche containing thirty, which they carry with them always, so they are never unprepared.

When they have stayed long enough in one place, they deliberate where they shall go to try their luck. If any man happens to be familiar with particular coasts where the merchant-men trade, he offers his services. The trading-ships cruise to different places according to the season of the year, for these regions cannot be reached at all times on account of settled winds and currents. The people of New Spain and Campeche do most of their commerce in ships sailing in winter from Campeche to the coasts of Caracas, Trinidad and Margarita, as the north-east trade winds do not permit this voyage in summer. When summer comes, they turn their vessels homewards again. The privateers, knowing the passage through which they must sail, lie in wait for them.

If the rovers have been at sea a considerable time without accomplishing anything, they may take on desperate odds – and sometimes with success. For example, there was a buccaneer called Pierre François, of Dunkirk, who had been long at sea in a barque with a crew of twenty-six. He had been cruising in wait for ships coming from Maracaibo and bound for Campeche, but having missed his prey, he and his men resolved to go to Rancherías. This is a place lying off the mouth of the Rio de Hacha, at a latitude of $12\frac{1}{2}°$ north, where there are oyster-beds. Every year a fleet of ten to twelve barques, protected by a convoy-ship of twenty-four guns, comes from Cartagena to fish there for pearls. Every boat has two Negro divers, who go down four to six fathoms. François resolved to attack the pearl-fishers, and this is how he did it.

The boats lay at anchor on the pearl-bank, with the man-of-war about half a league away, towards the coast. The weather was calm so the buccaneers were able to approach without sails, like a Spanish coaster coming from Maracaibo. But when they drew near the oyster-beds, they rowed towards the flagship of the fleet, which was mounted with eight guns and had sixty well armed men aboard. As they came alongside, François ordered the flagship to surrender, but instead, she opened fire at once. After the broadside, the buccaneers opened fire so accurately that a number of the Spaniards fell, and before the flagship's gun-crews could reload, the rovers had clambered on board and compelled the Spaniards to cry for quarter.

They hoped the man-of-war would come to their aid, but François, to mislead the enemy, sank his own vessel and left the Spanish flag flying on the ship he had captured until he was ready to set sail. The Spaniards were sent below and the buccaneers put to sea. The man-of-war fired a victory salute, thinking the rovers had been defeated, but on seeing the ship move seawards, at once cut its cable and set off in pursuit. Dusk fell, and the warship was beginning to gain on the rover. The wind rose, but still the rover crammed on all sail, in order to escape. But misfortune overtook the fugitives, for the mainmast came crashing down to the deck, on account of the canvas the ship carried.

Nevertheless, the buccaneers' courage did not forsake them. They reloaded their muskets, tied the Spanish prisoners together two by two, and prepared to fight the man-of-war with only twenty-two men – for the rest of the crew had been wounded and were unfit for combat. They dropped the mainmast overboard and rigged as many sails as they could on the foremast and the bowsprit.

But at last the man-of-war overtook them and attacked so fiercely that François was forced to surrender, but on the terms that neither he nor his crew should be made to labour carrying lime or stones and that they should all be sent to Spain at the first opportunity. (When the Spaniards capture any buccaneers, they usually keep them three or four years at such labour, like slaves, only sending them back to Spain in the galleons when they have no more use for them.) These terms were granted, and François gave up the booty with infinite regret, as it included pearls to the value of 100,000 pieces of eight, for the entire catch of all the fleet had been on board. This would have been an immense prize for the rover had he been able to keep it – which doubtless would have been the case if the mainmast had not split.

Here is another example, which began no less boldly and ended no less unluckily. A man known as Bartolomeo el Portugues sailed from Jamaica in a barque mounting four guns and thirty men. Rounding Cabo de Corrientes on the island of Cuba, he saw a ship approaching, come from Maracaibo and Cartagena and bound for Havana and thence for Hispaniola. This ship carried twenty guns and other armament, and had seventy people on board, passengers as well as seamen. The buccaneers resolved to board her and carried out the attempt with great courage, but were bravely beaten back by the Spaniards. On the second attempt they took the ship, with a loss of ten dead and four wounded, although the Spaniards still had forty men alive, counting those fit for service and the wounded.

The buccaneers could not return to Jamaica as the wind was against them, so decided to make for Cabo San Antonio (in the western corner of Cuba) as they were short of water. Near the cape they encountered three ships, come from New Spain and bound for Havana. These ships came alongside, forced the rovers to give up their plunder and moreover took them all prisoner. It grieved them no little, having to hand over

77

such precious booty – for the ship had been laden with 120,000 pounds of cacao, and had 70,000 pieces of eight on board.

Two days after their capture, the ships were separated in a huge gale which blew up, and the trading-ship where the buccaneers were held prisoner touched in at Campeche. Various traders came on board the merchantman to welcome the captain. These men knew Bartolomeo, the rovers' chief, for he had inflicted terrible havoc along this coast, murdering people and burning houses.

Next day, the town's officers of justice came on board asking the captain to hand over the buccaneers, a demand which he dared not refuse. But as the townspeople feared the pirate chief might give them the slip – as he had frequently done before – they made Bartolomeo remain on board ship while they erected a gallows on which to hang him next morning. Bartolomeo spoke good Spanish, and overheard the sailors discussing the hanging. He at once looked for some means of saving his life. He took two empty wine-jars and stoppered them tightly with cork. That night, when everyone was asleep except the sentry who stood guarding him, Bartolomeo did all he could to persuade the man to go to his hammock. But as he showed no intention of doing so, Bartolomeo decided to cut his throat. This he did, without giving the sentry a chance to cry out. Immediately Bartolomeo lowered himself gently into the water with his two jars, and with their help swam to the shore. He made for the forest, where he hid himself for three days before deciding on any course of action.

Early next morning soldiers were sent to patrol the shore, where they guessed he might be. But Bartolomeo was too cunning for them. He watched their movements from the shelter of the woods, and only when they returned to the city began making his way along the coast towards El Golfo Triste (about thirty leagues from Campeche). He reached this place at last, after a journey of fourteen days – not without much hardship from hunger and thirst and the discomforts of travel. He dared not take the main road for fear of falling into the hands of the Spaniards. For four days he was laboriously clambering through the thickets of trees which grow along the shore, with as many roots in the water as branches up above, without setting a foot on the ground. During those four days he had nothing but a small calabash of water, and ate nothing except periwinkles which he pulled off the rocks.

To make matters worse, he had to cross several rivers, though he could hardly swim – yet a man desperately trying to save his life will undertake hazards another would not dream of. He found an old plank washed up on the beach, with some big nails sticking out of it. These he hammered flat with stones, and ground their edges until they were sharp enough to cut with. Then he hacked down creepers and bound together pieces of driftwood he had gathered, and so made a raft on which to cross the rivers.

Finally he came to Triste, where he found a buccaneers' ship from Jamaica. When he had told them his adventures, he urged them to give him a canoe and twenty men, to make a surprise attack by night on the ship where he had been a prisoner, at anchor in Campeche. The buccaneers agreed. Eight days later, Bartolomeo and his twenty men arrived at dead of night at Campeche harbour, and instantly, without speaking a word, boarded the ship. The men on the ship had thought it was one of the canoes from the city carrying contraband – but they soon found their mistake when the buccaneers all leapt on board and captured the vessel. The rovers immediately cut the anchor cable and set sail. There was still plenty of merchandise on board, but the gold had been taken out.

Bartolomeo el Portugues now forgot all the hardships he had suffered, for he had a good ship once more, with high hopes of making his fortune. But just when he thought he was on top of all his difficulties, the ill-luck which constantly dogged him brought him down again in a short time. He had set his course for Jamaica and was sailing in the region of the Isle of Pines, to the south of Cuba, when his ship ran aground on the reefs of Los Jardines, in a southerly gale. With bitter heartache, he and his men had to abandon ship and flee in their canoe to Jamaica. They did not linger there, but soon made ready to go off in quest of booty once again – yet fortune always went against el Portugues. He made many violent attacks on the Spaniards without gaining much profit from marauding, for I saw him dying in the greatest wretchedness in the world.

There is a buccaneer still living in Jamaica whose exploits have been no less bold. He was born in Groningen, and lived for a long time in Brazil, but when the Portuguese retook that country from the Dutch, various settlers there had to leave. Some went to Holland, others to the French or English islands, and some to the Virgin Isles. This man went to Jamaica, and not knowing what else to do, joined the buccaneers, who called him Rock the Brazilian. First he shipped as a common seaman, and became very popular with the crew. A party of malcontents rallied to his side and parted company with their captain, taking a barque, of which they made Rock the captain.

Soon they captured a ship from New Spain, with much money on board, and brought it to Jamaica. Rock acquired great renown from this exploit, and in the end became so audacious he made all Jamaica tremble. He had no self-control at all, but behaved as if possessed by a sullen fury. When he was drunk, he would roam the town like a madman. The first person he came across, he would chop off his arm or leg, without anyone daring to intervene, for he was like a maniac. He perpetrated the greatest atrocities possible against the Spaniards. Some of them he tied or spitted on wooden stakes and roasted them alive between two fires, like killing a pig – and all because they refused to show him the road to the hog-yards he wanted to plunder.

Once he was cruising after prey along the coast of Campeche when his ship ran aground in a storm. He and his crew had to abandon ship and make for the shore, without being able to rescue anything but their muskets and some powder and shot. This occurred between Campeche and Triste. Straight away they hurried towards El Golfo Triste, where the rovers always put in to repair their ships. After three or four days they were worn out with hunger and thirst and the rough road, so that they could hardly go another step – but worst of all, they were observed by a party of a hundred Spanish cavalry who chanced to come that way.

Captain Rock urged his comrades on, saying he had no intention of giving himself up, but would rather die than be taken prisoner by the Spaniards. The rovers were thirty in number, all well armed, and as their captain had put good heart into them, resolved to die with him rather than surrender. Meantime, the Spaniards were riding violently down on them. The rovers let them approach until they could not miss their aim, and every bullet found its mark. The battle went on for an hour, when the surviving Spaniards took flight. The buccaneers killed the wounded Spaniards instantly, and took their horses and the food they had been carrying. They could now proceed on their way with ease, without having lost more than two of their mates killed, and two wounded.

They rode on horseback along the coast road, and before they arrived at the Gulf, they noticed a Spanish barque off shore, come to cut logwood. The rovers turned back, sending out six of their men in advance to spy on the enemy's movements. In the morning, when the Spaniards came on shore, these men took their canoe and all six jumped on board, rowed out to the barque and captured it as well. As there were few provisions on the vessel, they slaughtered some of their horses and salted the flesh with salt they found on board, to live on till they came across better fare.

Not long after this, the buccaneers captured a ship come from New Spain, laden with meal and many pieces of eight, which had been bound for Maracaibo to purchase cacao. Captain Rock sailed for Jamaica with this prize, and lorded it there with his mates until all was gone. For that is the way with these buccaneers – whenever they have got hold of something, they don't keep it for long. They are busy dicing, whoring and drinking so long as they have anything to spend. Some of them will get through a good two or three thousand pieces of eight in a day – and next day not have a shirt to their back. I have seen a man in Jamaica give 500 pieces of eight to a whore, just to see her naked. Yes, and many other impieties.

My own master often used to buy a butt of wine and set it in the middle of the street with the barrel-head knocked in, and stand barring the way. Every passer-by had to drink with him, or he'd have shot them dead with a gun he kept handy. Once he bought a cask of butter and threw the stuff at everyone who came by, bedaubing their clothes or their head, wherever he best could reach.

The buccaneers are generous to their comrades: if a man has nothing, the others will come to his help. The tavern-keepers let them have a good deal of credit, but in Jamaica one ought not to put much trust in these people, for often they will sell you for debt, a thing I have seen happen many a time. Even the man I have just been speaking about, the one who gave the whore so much money to see her naked, and at that time had a good 3,000 pieces of eight – three months later he was sold for his debts, by a man in whose house he had spent most of his money.

But to return to our tale. Captain Rock soon squandered all his money, and was obliged to put to sea again with his mates. He went back to the coast of Campeche, which was his usual place for marauding. After barely fourteen days there, he went off in a canoe to reconnoitre the shipping in the road-stead of Campeche to see if he could take a vessel. But his ill-luck decreed that he himself should be captured by the Spaniards, together with his canoe and ten of his comrades besides.

He was instantly brought before the governor, who had him shut up in a dark hole with little to eat. The governor would gladly have had him hanged, but dare not, because the buccaneer had thought of a crafty ruse. He wrote a letter to the governor, as if it had come from his comrades among the other buccaneers, threatening they would show no mercy in future however many Spaniards they took, if the governor did Rock any harm.

The governor, on receiving this letter, feared he himself might share such a fate, for previously Campeche had almost fallen into the hands of the rovers, under the leadership of a certain Mansveldt [*sic*] who had been a celebrated buccaneer of Jamaica. The governor therefore decided to send Captain Rock to Spain with the galleons. He made the buccaneer promise on his oath that he would never more return to piracy, threatening he would hang him without mercy if Rock ever fell into his clutches again.

Captain Rock had not been long in Spain before he was on the look-out for a chance of returning to Jamaica. On the journey from the West Indies he had gained some 500 pieces of eight by fishing, with which he bought clothes and other necessaries, and back he went to the island. Having arrived in Jamaica, he set about the work of marauding with more cunning and boldness than ever, devoting all his energy to every exploit which promised to harm the Spaniards.

The Spaniards, seeing there was no getting rid of the buccaneers, were driven to reduce the number of their voyages – but this did them no good. When the buccaneers were unable to capture their ships at sea, they gathered together and came on land, plundering many villages and towns. The rover who initiated these land attacks was Lewis Scot. He took the town of Campeche, plundered the place and forced the citizens to pay ransom before abandoning it. After him came Mansveldt, who undertook to land in New Granada and ravage as far as the South Sea – which in fact he did, but was forced to turn back eventually from lack of food. First he captured the island of St Catalina, where he took some prisoners who set him on the way to the city of Cartagena.

Another buccaneer – John Davis of Jamaica – led a daring enterprise in this same territory. For a long time he had been lurking in the Gulf of Boca del Toro, on the look-out for ships from Cartagena bound for Nicaragua, but had missed them. He and his men decided to leave their ship in the mouth of the Nicaragua river and make their way upstream in canoes, to arrive at the city by night and plunder the churches and the property of the principal merchants. They were a band of ninety strong, and had three canoes among them. Leaving ten men on the ship, which was concealed among the trees at the river mouth so as not to be seen by Indians coming to fish, all the rest took to the canoes. They travelled upriver by night, hiding by day under the trees along the bank.

At about midnight on the third night they reached the town. The sentry took them for fishers from the lagoon, for several of the rovers spoke good Spanish. Also, they had an Indian with them who used to live there and had fled because the Spaniards wanted to make him a slave. This Indian sprang on shore, approached the sentry and murdered him. Then they all landed and paid a visit to the mansions of three or four of the principal citizens. They took all the money they could lay hands on, and also robbed several churches, but by this time some fugitives who had managed to escape their clutches were setting up an outcry through the town.

The citizens and the garrison began to rouse up, so the rovers were compelled to flee, carrying off as much loot as they could manage. They also took along a few prisoners, to use them to obtain quarter, should they be overtaken.

As soon as they reached the river mouth, the rovers made ready their ship with the utmost speed and put to sea. They had made the prisoners, for their ransom, procure them as much meat as was needed for the return journey to Jamaica. While they were still in the mouth of the river, some 500 armed Spaniards rode up, but the buccaneers' bold cannon-fire repelled them. To their great ignominy, the Spaniards had to watch them sail away with their goods. Ninety rovers had dared to land, reach a town more than forty leagues from the shore and garrisoned by a good 800 men, and in so short a time had carried off such splendid booty. The buccaneers had taken over 40,000 pieces of eight in ready money, as well as silver and jewels.

Soon afterwards they came with their loot back to Jamaica,

where they promptly squandered it all, so once more they had to go in quest of prey. John Davis was chosen by a group of rovers as chief of their seven or eight ships, as he was a good leader. They resolved to cruise along the north coast of Cuba to lie in wait for the fleet from New Spain and plunder some of its ships. This plan did not succeed, yet, rather than return home without booty, they decided to sail for the coast of Florida. Here they landed and took a small town called San Augustin. This town had a fort, garrisoned by two companies of soldiers, yet despite this the rovers plundered the place and got away without the Spaniards being able to do them any injury.

PART TWO

*The origins of the renowned buccaneers,
François l'Olonnais and John Morgan,*
and their most celebrated exploits
against the Spaniards in America;
together with the life and deeds
of certain other sea-rovers living
in and around these regions.*

*

* *Translator's note:*
This famous Morgan's name was Henry,
and the buccaneer called l'Olonnais
was Jean-David Nau.

CHAPTER ONE

*Origin of François l'Olonnais and beginning of
his marauding.*

FRANÇOIS L'OLONNAIS was born at a place called Les
Sables d'Olonne on the French coast. He was shipped out to
the Caribbean Islands as a boy in the usual way, as an indentured servant or slave. When he had served his time, he
stayed among the hunters on Hispaniola for a period. Later
on he took to robbing the Spaniards, gaining immense booty
and committing unspeakable atrocities. I will describe the
main exploits of his career, up to his death.

After he had made two or three voyages with the buccaneers, always showing great courage, the governor of
Tortuga, M. de la Place, gave him command of a ship with
which to plunder and seek his fortune, for at that time there
was war between France and Spain. With this vessel, l'Olonnais gained enormous spoils, but his cruelties made him
notorious among the Spaniards, his infamy raising a clamour
throughout the entire region. Whenever they encountered him
at sea, they fought till they could fight no more, for he
granted Spaniards little mercy.

Fortune, favourable to him for so long, now began to turn
her back on him. He had the great ill-luck to lose his ship
in a northerly gale on the coast of Campeche. He and his crew
were forced to go ashore to save their lives. The Spaniards
saw them and attacked, killing most of the men. L'Olonnais
knew there would be no mercy for him either, and there was
no chance of escape, as he was already wounded. He smeared
himself with blood and crept under the corpses lying on the
beach. When the enemy had left the battlefield, he withdrew
to the forest to think out how best to save his life.

Having recovered his strength and bound up his wounds,

l'Olonnais approached the outskirts of the city of Campeche, dressed in Spanish clothes. Here he spoke with some slaves, promising them freedom if they would follow his advice. The slaves listened to his words, stole one of their master's canoes, and put to sea with the buccaneer, sailing for Tortuga. The Spaniards, meanwhile, had thrown some of l'Olonnais' mates in prison, where they asked them what had become of their captain. The men replied that he was dead, for they knew no better. The Spaniards rejoiced and lit bonfires to celebrate this triumph, thanking God that it had pleased him to deliver them from such a cruel adversary.

Meanwhile, l'Olonnais had arrived in Tortuga in the canoe with the slaves. Far from applying himself to another trade, to avoid further perils of the kind he had just survived, the buccaneer was on the look-out for another ship. He put to sea once more with twenty well-armed men in a small vessel he had obtained by trickery, and made for a little town called De los Cayos, on the north shore of Cuba, where they export hides, tobacco and sugar to Havana. As it is very shallow along the coast, the Spaniards use barques for this trade.

L'Olonnais intended to plunder some of these vessels, but he was seen by some fishermen, who had the luck to escape him. These men went overland to Havana, crying out to the governor that l'Olonnais the French corsair was on the coast with two canoes, and they dare not pursue their trade for fear of him.

The governor did not believe it, for he had received letters from Campeche, saying l'Olonnais was dead. Nevertheless, at the entreaty of the Spaniards who brought the news, he had a small ship made ready, mounted with ten guns and carrying ninety well-armed men. This ship was dispatched with orders not to return without having destroyed the rovers. To carry out this intention, he sent along a Negro to be executioner and hang the buccaneers – except their chief, who was to be brought to Havana.

The ship arrived before the town of De los Cayos – but instead of its going to seek out the marauders, the buccaneers came looking for the Spaniards. Some fishermen whom they had captured had told them where the ship was and what her intentions were, hoping by this news to scare the rovers away from the coast. On the contrary – l'Olonnais had such an avid desire to get a ship, to enable him to wreak greater havoc and make a bigger fortune, that he and his crew resolved to tackle the man-of-war.

The Spanish ship lay in an estuary, and the buccaneers forced one of the captured fishermen to guide them to her, proceeding inshore under cover of the trees. At two o'clock at night the buccaneers came up with the Spaniards, who hailed them, asking if they had seen the corsairs. The buccaneers answered, 'No – warned of your coming, they have fled.' The men in the ship of war had good reason to think otherwise when, next morning, still without being able to see the buccaneers, they heard their warlike greeting.

The Spaniards immediately took up battle stations, firing both broadsides as there was a pirate canoe near each bank of the river. When the Spaniards had fired two or three salvoes, the buccaneers judged the right moment had come and swarmed on board all together, cutlass in hand, and chased all the Spaniards below deck. L'Olonnais let them come up one after the other, and as they came through the hatch, struck off their heads. When he had finished off a number of them, there came the turn of the Negro who was to have been the rovers' executioner. '*Señor capitan,*' he cried, '*No me mateis – os diré la verdad!*' (That is: 'Don't kill me – I will tell you the truth!')

L'Olonnais heard his confession, and then carried on as before, killing all the remaining Spaniards except one. He gave this man a letter for the governor of Havana and a verbal message declaring that, however many Spaniards he captured, he would give no quarter. At the same time l'Olonnais also made a vow to kill himself rather than ever surrender into the hands of the Spaniards. The letter contained similar statements, and also said that l'Olonnais hoped to do the same to the governor of Havana as he would have done to him.

When he received the news of this disaster, the governor was enraged beyond measure, and swore death to every buccaneer who should fall into his hands. But the inhabitants of Cuba all begged him to do no such thing. They had to put to sea every day to seek their livelihood, and the rovers could capture a hundred of them for every buccaneer the Spaniards might take, therefore they implored the governor not to set such revengeful hostility in motion.

L'Olonnais had now managed to get the ship he wanted, but he found little booty on board, so decided to pick up more men here and there and go cruising for prey. This he did, with good success, for he captured a ship in Maracaibo Bay bound for Maracaibo to buy cacao, with plenty of money and merchandise on board. Then he returned to Tortuga, amid great rejoicing. He had not been there long before he resolved to form a fleet to go and raid the Spanish coast. He had taken some prisoners who promised to be his guides, providing he could get together a force of 500 men. The rovers' intention was to take Maracaibo and plunder all the villages and towns along the entire coast. The prisoners were very familiar with the region, in particular a Frenchman who had a wife there.

CHAPTER TWO

*L'Olonnais equips a fleet to raid the Spanish
coasts of America.*

L'OLONNAIS sent word of his intention to all the buccaneers.
Within two months he had gathered 400 men together, and
was ready to begin. Another free-booter living on the island
was Michel the Basque, a man who had won so much by
marauding he no longer went to sea. However, seeing the
chance of huge spoils if l'Olonnais' plans succeeded, this man
made friends with the buccaneer leader and offered him his
services, saying he was capable of commanding men on land
in all eventualities. In view of his experience with the army in
Europe, l'Olonnais made him commander of his forces on
land. The expedition embarked in eight vessels, l'Olonnais'
small ship, which mounted ten guns, being the biggest of
them all.

When all was ready, they set sail from Tortuga at the end of
April – a force of 660 men. They made for a place called
Bayaha, on the north coast of Hispaniola, where they took on
board a party of hunters, together with all the provisions
needed for the voyage.

At the end of July they were sailing towards Punta de
Espada, the eastern point of the island, when they caught
sight of a ship from Puerto Rico, bound for New Spain
with a cargo of cacao. Giving orders for his fleet to await him
on the island of Savona, to the south, Admiral l'Olonnais
pursued this ship on his own.

After a chase of two hours, the Spanish ship turned broadside on, well equipped to do battle. Nevertheless, after two or
three hours' combat, the ship was taken. The vessel mounted
sixteen guns and had fifty fighting men on board. The rovers
found she carried 120,000 pounds of cacao, and 40,000 pieces of

eight in ready money, as well as jewels to the value of 10,000 pieces of eight at least. L'Olonnais sent the ship to Tortuga to be unloaded, with orders that as soon as the cargo was out the vessel was to return and join him at Savona.

When l'Olonnais and the rest of his fleet arrived at Savona they met a ship come from Comana, with munitions of war and money to pay the garrison at San Domingo. They took this ship without firing a shot: she was mounted with eight guns, and had on board 7,000 pounds of gunpowder, a quantity of muskets and fuses, and 12,000 pieces of eight. This was an excellent beginning, and it gave the buccaneers great encouragement to find their fleet so strongly reinforced from the start.

When the ship with the cacao arrived at Tortuga, the governor had it unloaded immediately, had fresh provisions put on board with the utmost speed, and sent it back to l'Olonnais at the rendezvous. Within a fortnight, the vessel reached Savona. L'Olonnais embarked on this ship himself, and gave his old ship to his comrade, Antony du Puis. He had recruited some more men to replace those killed and wounded in capturing the ship, so his fleet was now in good condition, with every man eager to fight for booty.

When all was ready they set sail, steering for Maracaibo Bay. This bay lies on the mainland coast of New Venezuela, about latitude 12° north; it is some twenty leagues deep and twelve leagues across. To seaward of the bay lie the islands of Onega and Monges; the eastern headland of the bay is called Cabo San Roman, and the western, Cabo Coquibacoa. This bay generally goes by the name of the Gulf of Venezuela, but the buccaneers call it Maracaibo Bay.

In the strait giving access to the interior part of the bay are two islets. The easterly one is called Isla de la Vigia, or Lookout Island, because on a high hill in the middle stands a watchtower, with a sentinel on duty day and night. The other is called Isla de las Palomas, or Pigeon Island. Beyond these islets, deeper inland, is a lake of sweet water, sixty leagues by thirty. This lake flows through the strait into the Gulf of

Venezuela and the open sea. The entrance for shipping between the two islets is no wider than the range of an eight-pounder. On Pigeon Island stands a fort guarding the strait, as any ship wishing to enter the lake must pass close to the island. For at the mouth is a bar, or sandbank, in fourteen feet of water, and about a league inwards is another sandbank called El Tablazo, where there is only ten feet of water. Thereafter, as far as Rio de las Espinas (about forty leagues along the lake) the water is six, seven and eight fathoms deep.

Some six leagues along the lake shore, on the western side, lies Maracaibo, a very handsome city with fine-looking houses along the waterfront. The population is considerable: counting the slaves, it is reckoned that three or four thousand souls live there, and among them 800 men capable of bearing arms, all Spaniards. There are four monasteries, a hospital and a great parish church. The city is ruled by a deputy governor, subordinate to the governor of Caracas; the chief trade is in hides and tallow. The citizens are rich in cattle, and also have plantations on the other side of the lake, some thirty leagues south of Maracaibo, around a big village called Gibraltar. Here cacao is grown in great quantity, as well as all kinds of crops to provide food for Maracaibo, as the land around that city is very dry and infertile. Every day boats cross from Gibraltar laden with produce such as lemons, oranges, melons and vegetables of every kind. These boats take back meat from Maracaibo, as the land around Gibraltar is unsuitable for rearing cattle and sheep.

The city has an excellent harbour, with facilities for building as many ships as they please, though the timber has to be brought down from the hinterland. Facing the city is a small islet called Isla Borica where many goats are reared, but only for the skins and tallow, for they seldom eat the meat, apart from that of the kids. Many sheep are kept around Maracaibo, and inland are numerous fields, but the ground is barren and dry. The animals are all small, a sign of scant grazing.

There are tribes of Indians living along the western shore, still unconquered, whom the Spaniards call Indios Bravos. They will have no dealings with the Spaniards. They build their houses high up in the trees which grow in the water, so as to be less plagued by the mosquitoes. On the eastern side of the lake are Spanish fishing villages, built on piles above the water. The surrounding land is so low and swampy the mosquitoes make life intolerable, and there is danger of floods. The lake is fed by seventy-five rivers and streams, and when it rains hard the land may be flooded for a distance of two or three leagues. The village of Gibraltar often lies so deep under water that the inhabitants are forced to abandon their houses and retreat inland to the plantations.

Gibraltar is situated at the waterside, forty leagues along the lake shore. About 1,500 people live there, including 400 men capable of bearing arms, mostly shopkeepers and tradesmen. Around the village are many plantations of cacao and sugar-cane. The land is very fertile and full of fine trees, providing timber for houses and ship-building. One finds immense cedars, forty feet in girth, from which they make dug-out vessels called *piraguas*, which can carry a topsail.

Beautiful rivers flow through all the surrounding country-side. Cacao plantations grow beside the rivers, and in time of drought they channel water into these plantations along ditches, which have sluices to check the flow when they have sufficient. Considerable quantities of tobacco are also produced, of a kind highly esteemed in Europe; this is the genuine Virginian tobacco, known as Pope's Tobacco.

The fertile land stretches some twenty leagues, being bounded on the lake side by swamps and on the other by high mountains, always covered with snow. On the far side of the mountains is a large town called Merida, having authority over the village of Gibraltar. Merchandise from Gibraltar is taken there over the mountains on pack-mules – and this only once a year, because the journey is so cold as to be almost unbearable. On the return journey from Merida they bring back meal, sent from Peru by way of Santa Fé.

A Spaniard told me of a sort of people who live in these mountains, of the same stature as the Indians, but with short curly hair and with long claws on their feet, like apes. Their skin resists arrows and all sharp instruments, and they are very agile climbers, having tremendous strength. The Spaniards attempted to kill some of the tribe with their lances, but the iron could not pierce their tough skin. These wild men managed to seize some of the Spaniards, carrying them up to the tree-tops and hurling them to the ground. These people have never been heard to speak. Sometimes they come down to the plantations at the foot of the mountains and carry off any women slaves they can capture.

I have read various descriptions of America, but never found any mention of such people, so I believe they must be a sort of Barbary ape living in those parts, for I have seen many apes in the forest. Nevertheless, several Spaniards have assured me that these creatures are human, and that they have seen them frequently: I give it here for what it's worth. Truly, God's works are great, and these things may well be.

I have described the environs of Lake Maracaibo so the reader may have a better understanding of the events which follow. Having arrived in the Gulf of Venezuela, l'Olonnais and his fleet lay at anchor, out of sight of the watch on Look-out Island. Early next day they moved to the mouth of Lake Maracaibo, dropping anchor in front of the sand-bar. They could not enter the lake without passing close under el Fuerte de la Barra, so l'Olonnais landed his men in order to attack this fort. It consisted only of a battery of sixteen cannon surrounded by several gabions, or earth-filled wicker cylinders, with a ramp of earth thrown against them to shelter the men inside.

The buccaneers, who had landed about a league away, began their advance on the fort. The fort commandant had placed an ambush of soldiers to take the rovers from the rear and throw them into disarray while he launched a frontal assault. But the buccaneers had sent out an advance guard of fifty men, who discovered the ambush and attacked the soldiers, cutting off their retreat to the fort. Meanwhile the main body came up and attacked. Within three hours they had captured the fort, with no other arms than their muskets.

Spaniards from the ambuscade had fled to Maracaibo, where they astounded the citizens with the news that the corsairs were on their way with a force of two thousand men. Maracaibo had been plundered by rovers ten or twelve years ago, an event still fresh in the minds of the citizens. Everybody began packing, ready to move out. Those who had vessels loaded their property aboard and made for Gibraltar, where they spread the news that the corsairs were come and el Fuerte de la Barra captured. Those without boats sent their goods inland on horses and pack-mules.

As soon as they had taken the fort, the buccaneers hoisted their flag, as a sign that the ships of their squadron could enter. They spent the rest of the day demolishing the fort, burning the gun-carriages, spiking the guns, carrying their wounded on board their ships and burying their dead. Early next morning the fleet set sail for Maracaibo, about six leagues away. All day long the weather was calm and they could only advance with the tide, so their progress was slow.

They reached the city early the following morning, and at once ranged their vessels so that the landing could be made under covering fire from the ships' cannons. They expected the Spaniards to have men hidden in the thickets along the beach. As the buccaneers approached the shore in their canoes, the ships discharged their cannons. Half the raiders sprang on shore, while the other half stayed in the canoes, firing into the trees – but they received no answer.

When the buccaneers entered the city they found it deserted, for all the Spaniards had fled with their wives and children. Nevertheless, they found all sorts of foodstuffs in the houses, together with wine and brandy and plenty of hens, pigs, bread and meal. Then the buccaneers began to make merry with great eagerness: they had been leading a sober life for a long time, and had not cast eyes on such good things for months. The best houses in the town were taken over as quarters for the troops. Sentries were posted, and the great church was turned into a guardhouse.

Next morning a party of 150 men was sent out to try to take prisoners, so as to find out where the citizens had hidden their wealth. The expedition returned in the evening, bringing with them about 20,000 pieces of eight, several mules laden with various goods, and some twenty prisoners – men, women and children. Next day they put some of the prisoners to the rack to find if they knew the whereabouts of other hidden stores, but nobody wanted to tell tales.

L'Olonnais – who cared nothing for the death of a dozen or so Spaniards – drew his cutlass and hacked one of the prisoners to pieces before their very eyes, vowing he would do the same to them all if they would not tell what they knew. One prisoner was so terrified by his threats he promised to lead the buccaneers to where the citizens were hiding. But the fugitives, realizing the prisoners would peach on them, had buried their goods underground, and every day fled from one hiding-place to another. The rovers had no means of running them to earth, except by chance in the search. The citizens were so fearful of one another that a father would not trust his own son.

After being in Maracaibo fourteen days, the buccaneers resolved to move on to Gibraltar. The Spaniards, whose spies had reported the strength of the enemy forces, had already sent a boat to Gibraltar warning the people that the rovers intended to land there and then march on Merida. Immediately, an express messenger rode over the mountains to inform their governor of what had happened.

The governor of Merida, who had seen much service in Flanders as a colonel, felt confident he could subdue the corsairs with little difficulty. He entered Gibraltar with some 400 well-armed men, and at once ordered the citizens to take up arms. On mustering these men, he found them to be about 400 strong, so that with his own troops he had a force of 800. Then he mounted a battery on the shore with twenty-two cannon, protected by gabions, together with a redoubt mounting eight guns. He blocked the main road along the shore, the only other way to the town being an almost impassable track through the swamps, where the mud came up to a man's knees.

The buccaneers, who knew nothing of these preparations, had embarked their prisoners and all the loot taken from Maracaibo, and were sailing towards Gibraltar. When they came in sight of the place they saw the flag waving above the village and many people on the shore.

L'Olonnais, as chief of the buccaneers, held council with his deputies and then with all his men. This time, he warned, they would have hot iron to handle: the Spaniards had long been forewarned of their presence in the lake, and had rallied a strong force to oppose them. Then he declared his own opinion: 'If they are strong, so much the more booty for us when we have gained the victory.' All the buccaneers voted in agreement, saying they would rather fight in the hope of good spoils than have travelled so far to get nothing. L'Olonnais answered, 'I will lead you – and the first man to show lack of courage in the battle, I will shoot him down.'

Having made their resolve, the buccaneers anchored close to the coast about a quarter of a league from the town. Next morning at sunrise, l'Olonnais landed all his forces – they were 380 strong, every man with a good musket and a cartouche at his side holding thirty cartridges, together with a pistol or two and a good cutlass. After the men had shaken hands all round and sworn oaths to stand by each other till death, l'Olonnais began the advance, crying, '*Allons, mes frères, suivez-moi, et ne faites point les lâches.*' ('Come on, brothers, follow me and let's have no cowardice.')

With this, forth they marched, ready for the attack. But when they reached the road their guide had pointed out, they found it blocked. They had to take the other track through the marshes, where the Spaniards could shoot them at their pleasure. Nevertheless, the buccaneers refused to be daunted. They pulled out their cutlasses and hacked down branches to fill up the path, so as not to sink so deep in the mud. All this time the Spaniards kept up a continuous fire. The rovers could hardly see or hear one another, what with the smoke and the roar of the guns.

At last they reached firm ground, where they found themselves faced with six cannons loaded with grape-shot and musket bullets. After discharging their cannons, the Spaniards made a sortie, but met with such a ferocious reception from the buccaneers that few managed to get back inside the earthworks. But the great guns kept up such a withering fire that many of the rovers lay dead or wounded. The rest tried to break through the forest by other paths, but with no luck, for the Spaniards had cut down huge trees and barred every way. Yet, despite all their adversities, the buccaneers never lost heart, but kept up a continuous, strong fire.

The Spaniards dared attempt no more sorties, and the rovers were unable to scale the gabions. Seeing this stalemate, l'Olonnais remembered a stratagem which might deceive the Spaniards. He and his men pretended to retreat. No sooner did the Spaniards see this withdrawal than about 200 of them rushed out pell-mell to attack. Once they had lured them out, the buccaneers instantly turned. After firing their muskets, they took cutlass in hand and fell upon the Spaniards, striking most of them dead. In their fury they trampled on the corpses and surged over the gabions, putting all the Spaniards behind the earthworks to flight and pursuing them into the forest, where they killed every man they found. The Spaniards manning the redoubt gave themselves up, on condition they would be given quarter.

The buccaneers at once tore down the Spanish flags, and took prisoner everyone they found in the village, herding them all inside the great church. They brought up most of the cannons and mounted them behind a breastwork, not knowing what might be in store for them. They expected the Spaniards would rally their forces and try to drive them out.

But on the next day, the buccaneers knew they had no reason to be afraid. When they came to gather the corpses for burial, so as to cause no stench, they found more than 500 Spanish dead, not counting the wounded who had fled into the woods where they died from their injuries. As well as all these casualties, they had taken more than 150 male Spanish prisoners, as well as 500 women and children and slaves. Now all was calm, they counted their own losses, which proved to be forty dead and some thirty wounded. Most of these men died on account of the unhealthy atmosphere which brought on fever, and of their wounds soon turning gangrenous. The rovers flung all the Spanish dead into two old boats which lay on the beach, and took them out about a quarter of a league in the lake, where they sank them to the bottom.

The buccaneers gathered together all the money and stores they could find in the town, and then rested four or five days, without making any expeditions. During this time the Spaniards in the neighbourhood were hiding their wealth as well as they could. The rovers soon began to go out on the search again, bringing quantities of goods back to the town, as well as many slaves they found on the plantations. They had been in occupation about a fortnight when their prisoners began to die of hunger and discomfort, for the rovers had not come across much meat. There was plenty of flour, but the buccaneers were too lazy to bake bread for themselves, let alone for the Spaniards. Any sheep, pigs, cows or poultry they found they slaughtered for their own food, killing mules and donkeys for the Spaniards. Anyone who did not choose to eat such meat had to die of hunger, for the prisoners were given nothing else. The only people to get better fare were some of the women, whom the buccaneers used for their pleasure. Some they took by violence, and some of their own free will, driven to it by hunger. Those prisoners whom they suspected of having money were stretched on the rack; if they would not confess, the rovers killed them.

At last, after having been there about a month, they sent out four of their prisoners to warn the fugitive citizens they must pay a ransom of 10,000 pieces of eight within two days, or else the rovers would set the whole town on fire. When the time limit was up, the Spaniards still had not got the ransom ready, so the buccaneers started setting fire to the buildings. When the Spaniards realized the rovers were prepared to burn the whole town to ashes, they entreated them to put out the fires, promising that the money demanded should be brought. The rovers extinguished the fires – not however without damage to several houses, and a monastery church, which was burnt to the ground.

After receiving the ransom, the buccaneers embarked the loot they had plundered, together with a large group of slaves for whom no money had been paid (for all the prisoners had to be ransomed, and the slaves bought back again). They set sail for Maracaibo, where they found the Spaniards still in a state of consternation. They sent three or four prisoners whom they had taken in the previous assault on Maracaibo to inform the governor and citizens that they must send 30,000 pieces of eight to the ships to ransom the city, otherwise the buccaneers would burn down the whole place. In the meantime, they sent raiding parties on shore, who took all the statues, bells and paintings out of the churches and brought them back on board, as well as quantities of marine stores which they found in various warehouses.

The Spaniards who had been sent to demand the ransom returned with instructions to come to terms with the rovers. It was finally agreed the Spaniards should give 20,000 pieces of eight and 500 cattle, and once this was paid the rovers should make no more raids, but depart as soon as the beasts were slaughtered. This they did, to the great joy of the inhabitants, who wished them a more fervent adieu than they'd bid them welcome.

Three days after their departure from Maracaibo, back the rovers came again, to the utter amazement of the Spaniards, who were filled with fresh alarm. The reason was that they could not get one of their largest vessels – a ship they had captured – over the sandbank at the mouth of the lake, and had been compelled to come back to fetch a pilot. The Spaniards instantly agreed to this demand, to be rid of the rovers as quickly as possible, after their two months sojourn in the lake.

Having sailed out of the Gulf, the buccaneers set their course for Hispaniola, and after eight days arrived at Isla de la Vaca. This is a small island off the south coast, inhabited by a few French hunters, who sell the meat to the privateers when they call. n there. Here the rovers brought their spoils on shore and shared them out according to their custom. They calculated they had 260,000 pieces of eight in ready money, wrought silver and jewels. The silverware was weighed, being reckoned as ten pieces of eight to the pound; they assessed the jewels at various prices, having no exact knowledge of such things. Apart from this, there were at least 100 pieces of eight for every man in linen and silk goods, as well as other trifles. The wounded were first recompensed according to the system I have already explained. Then, after everyone had sworn an oath that he had kept nothing back for himself, every man was given his allotted payment. The share of those who had died in battle was given to their partners or friends.

Having divided the spoils, the buccaneers set sail for Tortuga, where they arrived with great joy a month later. For some the joy was short-lived – many could not keep their money three days before it was all gambled away. However, those who had lost what they had were helped by the others. A short time previously, three ships had arrived from France with cargoes of wine and brandy, so liquor was very cheap. But this did not continue for long: prices quickly went up, and soon the buccaneers were paying four pieces of eight for a flagon of brandy. Tortuga at that time was full of traders and dealers. The governor got the ship laden with cacao for a twentieth of what it was really worth. The tavern-keepers got part of their money and the whores took the rest, so once more the buccaneers – including l'Olonnais their chief – had to consider ways of obtaining more booty.

CHAPTER THREE

*L'Olonnais launches a new expedition to take
the towns of St Jago de Leon and Nicaragua,
where he dies in great misery.*

L'OLONNAIS had earned great renown in Tortuga for his
last voyage, which he had conducted with such profit and
success. However – as the proverb says – all the flood-tide
brings in, the ebb-tide carries away, so he was soon obliged
to attempt another enterprise. He had no difficulty in getting
men to join him; they were so allured by the previous exploit
they had no scruples about undertaking another. Moreover,
their confidence in l'Olonnais was so great they would have
followed him into the greatest peril in the world. Eventually,
after discussion with his lieutenants, l'Olonnais decided they
should enter Lake Nicaragua and plunder all the surrounding
towns and villages.

Having firmly resolved on this enterprise, l'Olonnais
assembled a force of some 700 men. Three hundred he put on
board the large vessel taken in Maracaibo; the rest he disposed on smaller ships, five in number, making a fleet of six
ships in all. Their rendezvous was on Hispaniola, at a place
called Bayaha, where they took on board salt meat for their
victuals.

Having drawn up their agreement and provisioned the
ships, they set sail for Matamano, on the south side of Cuba.
Their plan was to steal all the canoes they could find, for many
turtle-fishers live at this place, catching and salting turtles to
send to Havana. The buccaneers needed canoes to carry their
men upriver to Nicaragua, where it was too shallow for their
ships to navigate.

Having robbed these poor folk of their tools of trade and
also carried off some of the men themselves, the buccaneers

put to sea, steering for Cabo Gracias a Dios, situated on the mainland coast at a latitude of 15°, about 100 leagues from the Island of Pines. But they met with a calm, and drifted on the currents into the Gulf of Honduras. They did their best to regain their course, but wind and currents were against them, and l'Olonnais' great ship could not follow the others. Worst of all, they began to run short of food, so they were obliged to seek fresh supplies. At last, hunger drove them to make a landing at the first river mouth they came to. They sent a few canoes up the Rio Xagua, whose shores are inhabited by Indians. They pillaged all the Indian dwellings they could find, bringing back to their ships a quantity of Spanish wheat, which they call maize, together with pigs, poultry, turkeys, and everything they'd been able to lay hands on.

But this was still not enough to provision the buccaneers for the journey they had in mind, so they held another council, and decided to wait until the bad weather passed, in the meantime plundering all the towns and villages around the Gulf. So they cruised along the coast, seeking nothing but food supplies. Every place they came to they cleaned out so thoroughly the inhabitants themselves were left to go hungry, for the buccaneers devoured everything they could get hold of. They even shot the apes in the forest for food.

Eventually they came to Puerto Cavallo, where there are a few Spanish warehouses, in which are stored goods from inland, awaiting embarkation. Here they found and captured a Spanish merchant-ship, mounting twenty-four cannons and sixteen swivel-guns. The buccaneers went on shore, pillaging all they found and setting fire to the warehouses and the hides stored inside. They also took a number of prisoners, whom they treated most cruelly, inflicting on these poor folk every torment imaginable. When l'Olonnais had a victim on the rack, if the wretch did not instantly answer his questions he would hack the man to pieces with his cutlass and lick the blood from the blade with his tongue, wishing it might have been the last Spaniard in the world he had thus killed. And if one of the poor Spaniards, driven by fear and the cruel tortures he suffered, promised to lead the buccaneers to the citizens in hiding, and then through bewilderment could not find the way, he would be inflicted with a thousand torments – and then put to death at the end of it all.

After most of their prisoners had been done to death by the cruellest atrocities, the buccaneers at last found two who would lead them to a Spanish town called San Pedro, some ten or twelve leagues from Puerto Cavallo. L'Olonnais himself prepared to go there with 300 men, leaving the rest under the command of Moise van Wijn, and set off with the two guides.

Before they had advanced more than three leagues, they encountered a troop of Spaniards in ambush, who put up a fierce fight. Nevertheless, the buccaneers soon won the struggle, putting the Spaniards to flight. L'Olonnais questioned all the wounded as to the strength of the Spaniards, and put them to death when they would not blab. He had also taken a few unwounded prisoners, and questioned these men about the road ahead, and whether any further Spanish ambuscades had been laid. They said yes, there were more ambuscades.

L'Olonnais then took them aside one at a time, and asked if there were any other road to take to avoid the ambushes, and they each answered no. Then he brought them before all the other prisoners and again asked about the way. The men answered that they knew of no other road. Then l'Olonnais, being possessed of a devil's fury, ripped open one of the prisoners with his cutlass, tore the living heart out of his body, gnawed at it, and then hurled it in the face of one of the others, saying, 'Show me another way, or I will do the same to you.'

The wretched fellows, in enormous fear, promised they would show him another track, but said it was very difficult. Notwithstanding, in order to satisfy him, they led him another way, but it proved so inaccessible, L'Olonnais was forced to take the other road. '*Mor'dieu*,' he cried, in great rage, '*les bougres d'Espagnols me le payeront.*'

Next day they encountered a second ambush, which the

buccaneers attacked with such fury the Spaniards could not withstand for a single hour. L'Olonnais ordered his men to give no quarter. The more they killed on the way, he said, the less resistance they would find in the city. Thinking to weary the buccaneers with repeated assaults, the Spaniards retreated from one ambuscade to another.

Eventually, l'Olonnais came to the third ambush, which proved no greater impediment than the other two. Although this one was strongly placed, by throwing several hand grenades they forced the Spaniards to take flight. The buccaneers pursued them so vigorously that most were killed before they reached the city. Here the buccaneers were expected: the road along which they had to pass was blocked with strong barricades. There was no other way they could take to avoid these obstacles, as the town is set all around with thickets of *raquettes* or prickly pear, which are so full of spines it is impossible to push through them. They make a worse obstacle than the spiked caltrops which are used in Europe to obstruct the road where an army must pass.

When the Spaniards posted behind the barricades caught sight of the buccaneers, they set up a vigorous fire from their great guns. But the invaders dropped down flat on their bellies, and, when the volley had been discharged, attacked with muskets and hand grenades, inflicting great damage on the Spaniards. Yet this assault was not enough to enable them to break through, and they were forced to retire. They then made a fresh advance with few men, who held their fire until sure of their target, so that every shot killed or wounded a man.

Finally, towards evening, the Spaniards were forced to give up. They waved a white flag to call a parley. They surrendered the town, asking for quarter and for two hours' grace in which to remove some of their possessions elsewhere. This l'Olonnais granted. Thereupon the buccaneers entered the town, and for two hours made no interference, according to their promise. The Spaniards derived little profit from this respite, however, for as soon as the time was up the buc-

caneers were at their heels. They took all the goods and moreover made the fleeing Spaniards prisoners. Yet most of the
goods had been previously removed, and the buccaneers
found in the town nothing but some leather bags containing
indigo.

In the end, after having been there a few days and committed their usual atrocities, the rovers burned down the
town and moved out with what loot they'd been able to find.
On returning to the sea-shore, they found that their comrades,
who had stayed in the ships, had cruised along the coast and
had captured some Indian fishermen. These men had told
them that a ship from Spain was due to arrive at the Guatemala river. Leaving two canoes in the river mouth to keep a
look-out for this ship, the buccaneers crossed over to some
islands on the other side of the Gulf in order to careen their
ships and seek fresh food supplies, for there are many turtles
in those waters, very good to eat.

On arrival they split into parties, each group going to its
customary fishing ground. Everyone was busy making nets to
catch turtles. They make these nets from the fibrous bark of
macao trees, which they also use for making the ropes they
need on board ship. The buccaneers are never at a loss for
equipment, since they know how to make do with one material
or another. There are some islands, for example, where they
find pitch, used for making their boats watertight. And if
they need tar, they dilute the pitch with sharks' oil. This
pitch is washed up by the sea, in such huge quantities that
whole islands have been formed of it. It is not like the ships'
pitch we use in Europe, but is a certain scum from the sea
which naturalists call bitumen.

In my opinion, it comes from the wax thrown into the sea
in stormy weather and thence washed up on shore – for it is
mixed with sand, and has a smell like the black ambergris
which comes from the East. There are multitudes of bees in
these parts, making their honey in the forests, and it often
happens that a great storm will blow down the honeycombs
hanging from the trees and carry them seawards. Some

naturalists consider that the water effects a certain separation in this honey and wax, a separation which results in the formation of ambergris. This is easily credible, for when found the ambergris is still soft, and smells like wax.

The buccaneers careened their ships with the utmost speed, and held themselves in readiness for news of the arrival of the Spanish ship. In the meantime, they cruised in their canoes along the coast of Yucatan, where many Indians live, on the look-out for ambergris, which is thrown up on the off-shore islands. Since the buccaneers have brought us to this place, I will set down a few observations on these Indians, as their manner of life and their religion are noteworthy.

These Indians have been under Spanish dominion for over a hundred years, and whenever the Spaniards need their labour they carry them off, and treat them very cruelly. Every six months the Spaniards send a priest there, in order (so they make out) to convert the Indians – but the visit furnishes more ungodliness than honour and service to God, for they only come to rob these poor simple folk of what they possess.

When the priest arrives, the chief, whom they call *cacique*, has to give him his daughter or another woman of his family for the priest to use as long as he stays. Moreover, every day the Indians must give as many hens, as many eggs, as many turkeys – in short, as much of all they have – as the priest demands. Should they be caught practising their own religion, they are seized by the priest and his colleagues and punished. But when the priest sees they have nothing more to bring him, then he leaves – and as soon as he has gone, the Indians once more practise their own religion.

Each one of them has a god, whom he worships and prays to at his pleasure. When a child is born, the Indians immediately take it to the temple where they sacrifice daily to their gods. Here they strew ashes in a circle, having first passed them through a sieve so that no dirt is intermingled. The child is placed naked in the middle of the circle of ashes, where it remains the whole night. The temple is open on all sides, so that animals can wander in at will. Next morning, the child's relations come to look whether any animals have entered during the night, and if not, they leave the baby lying there until they can see that some creature has been around the child. This they can tell by the footprints, and the animal they perceive to have visited the child (be it cat or dog, horse or lion or whatever creature) they hold as the infant's patron, which will protect and help him in all adversity. In honour of this guardian they burn a sweet-smelling gum, known as copal.

When the child is old enough, his parents tell him whom he ought to worship, whereupon he goes to the temple and makes offerings to the particular beast they have indicated. When he has suffered any injury, or has had something stolen from him, he goes and makes a sacrifice to his patron, complaining of the one who had done him harm and seeking vengeance. Two or three days later, it frequently happens that the wrong-doer is found killed or mauled or bitten by an animal of the kind to whom the supplicant prayed. Thus we may see how these ignorant folk are misled and tormented by the devil.

A Spaniard told me a story relevant to this subject. This man had come to trade with the Indians. He was obliged to stay there a considerable time, and, since Spaniards are of such a nature they cannot live without women, he took himself an Indian wife, to look after him and for him to use for his pleasure (if one may call this pleasure). This Indian woman had gone to the plantations one day to fetch some fruit, and when she did not return promptly the Spaniard went there to see why she stayed so long. As he approached the plantation, he saw the Indian woman – and an animal, like a lion, doing his will with her. On seeing this the Spaniard was so astounded he immediately ran back to the house. As soon as the Indian woman came home again, he asked her what she had been doing with the lion he had seen near her. At first she seemed ashamed, and wanted to deny the occurrence, but at last she admitted it, saying that this lion was her patron. The Spaniard drove her from his house, and from then on would have no more to do with her.

These Indians inhabit all the islands lying in the Gulf of Honduras and the mainland coast of Yucatan, building their houses in various beautiful and remote places. They have no trust in each other, which drives them to make their plantations deep in the woods, hidden from their fellows. They also have unusual marriage ceremonies. For example, if an Indian desires to marry another's daughter, first he goes to ask her parents. The girl's father asks whether he has any other wife, and whether he has a large plantation, and is a good fisherman, and many other such questions. If all the answers are satisfactory, the father gives him a bow and arrow. Then the suitor goes at once to the girl, giving her a garland of plaited leaves and flowers which she must set on her head, throwing away the wreath she formerly wore (for it is the custom for girls who are still virgins to wear a braided garland on their heads). After this they go and make an offering to their patrons, asking that their wedding may come to pass.

Maize liquor is brewed at the girl's home, and all the friends gather together there. The father gives the girl to her suitor, and, being married, the bridegroom takes his bride away. Next day the girl comes to her mother and, tearing the wreath from her head, breaks it into pieces before her mother's feet, making a great outcry, as is their custom when a maid has lost her virginity. Then the husband comes with his weapons, and displays great friendship towards his bride's father. But now we will continue our story, and return to piracy.

The buccaneers had captured several canoes from the Indians on the island of Sambale, about five leagues from the coast of Yucatan. Ambergris is cast up on this island, when a storm has been blowing from the east. The currents bring all kinds of things to its shore – parts of canoes have been found from the Caribbean Islands, more than 500 leagues away. Between this island and the mainland the water is very shallow, so no large vessels can pass through. Both here and on the mainland is much Campeche wood, or logwood, and many other trees used in dyeing – which would be highly esteemed in Europe if we knew how to employ them. The Indians make extremely beautiful dyes from them, which do not fade like ours.

After the buccaneers had been there some three months, they received news of the Spanish ship they had been expecting. They embarked with the utmost speed and sailed to where the great ship lay at anchor, busy unloading. The buccaneers prepared to attack, but also sent some of their smaller vessels to lie in wait in the estuary for another barque which was due from upriver, laden with costly merchandise such as cochineal, indigo and silver.

The great ship was well provided with means of defence, the Spaniards having been warned that the corsairs were along the coast. Consequently, they had mounted forty-two cannon and other armament, as well as 130 men. L'Olonnais attacked with a ship bearing twenty-eight guns, and encountered such fierce resistance he had to draw off, together with another vessel which was supporting him. But meanwhile, under cover of the smoke of battle, four canoes came up full of buccaneers, who boarded the Spaniard and forced him to surrender.

However, the booty was not so great as they had anticipated, for the ship had been unloaded as fast as possible. Warned of the buccaneers' presence, the Spaniards had intended. after taking out the cargo, to anchor the ship in the river and await the corsairs' coming. Nevertheless, the buccaneers found fifty lasts of iron still on board, together with fifty of paper, a good number of full wine-jars and various other bales of goods, but of little value.

After capturing this ship, l'Olonnais held council with his whole fleet, proposing to go on to Guatemala. Some voted in favour, others could not agree. For many of them, this had been their first voyage with the buccaneers, and they'd thought pieces of eight were to be had just by shaking the trees. Now they were undeceived, and wanted to go back home. Others, who were used to this way of life, said they would rather starve than return without money.

The majority considered the voyage to Nicaragua would be unsuccessful, as most of the men were losing heart, and decided to separate from l'Olonnais. Moise van Klijn [previously called van Wijn] the man who had the ship taken in Puerto Cavallo, was among those who left, setting his course for Tortuga, where he intended to cruise. Another, Pierre le Picard, on seeing the others leave, decided to do the same. He sailed along the mainland coast to Costa Rica, where he made a landing at the river Veragua. He marched his men to a small town of the same name and pillaged the place, despite the resistance put up by the Spaniards, who had taken arms.

Le Picard and his men carried off several prisoners to their ship, but their plunder amounted to little, for Veragua is inhabited only by poor folk who work at the mines. There are several gold mines in the district, but these are not worked, except by slaves, who dig the earth out of the hills and wash it in the river. It commonly yields tiny pieces of gold the size of peas, sometimes bigger and sometimes smaller. All the rovers were able to find was about seven or eight pounds of gold.

Their intention had been to go farther on and plunder the town of Nata on the South Sea coast, where most of the merchants reside whose slaves work in Veragua. But le Picard's men could not achieve their object, as the Spaniards were in wait for them in great numbers.

L'Olonnais had stayed alone in the Gulf of Honduras, with the great ship he had taken from the Spaniards, in which he had 300 men. He would gladly have followed the others, but his ship was too heavy to beat up against wind and tide as the smaller vessels had done. Consequently, the men began to run short of food, so they had to come ashore seeking provisions, shooting monkeys and any kind of animals to eat.

Finally, after many hardships, l'Olonnais reached a group of islets called Islas de las Perlas, near Cabo Gracias a Dios. Among them are two larger islands, near which l'Olonnais ran his ship aground on a reef, having misjudged the depth. They all managed to get ashore in the canoes, removing the guns and unloading all the iron they had on board, but to no avail – the ship stuck fast. They decided to make a virtue of necessity and break up the ship as far as possible, in order to build a longboat out of the timber and iron.

While our rovers are engaged in this work, I will briefly describe these two islands, which are inhabited by people one might well call savages, as Christian men have never spoken with them nor found their dwellings. There are plenty who have passed six or seven months on these islands, yet have never been able to find where they live. These Indians have sturdy bodies, and are very quick runners and good divers. Once they hauled up a ship's anchor from the bottom, and it weighed a good six hundredweight. Their weapons are made entirely of wood, without any iron, but sometimes tipped with a shark's tooth. They do not shoot with a bow, as other Indians do, but use a special kind of lance, about nine feet long.

They have plantations in various parts of the forest, where they grow sweet potatoes, bananas, plantains, pineapples and other fruits of the country, but there are no houses near the plantation. It is said they eat human flesh. While l'Olonnais was there, one of his men went into the forest with only one companion, a Spaniard, and armed only with a musket. When they were a league or so in the wood, they were surprised by a troop of Indians. The Frenchman fired a shot and set off at a run, but the Spaniard was left behind, as he was not such a good runner. The first man reached the beach shortly after, but his companion was lost and never came out of the forest.

Some time later, a party of a dozen men, all well armed, entered the forest. The Frenchman was with them, and out of curiosity led them to where he had seen the Indians. Eventually they came upon a place where the Indians had lit a fire, and found there the bones of the missing Spaniard, together with a hand, which had been burnt and was half-eaten. They knew it was his hand, for the Spaniard had had only three fingers.

While they were in the forest they managed to capture four Indian women and five men, whom they took back to the shore. The buccaneers had some other Indians in their company who had lived in these regions; they asked these men to speak to the prisoners, but they could not understand one another. The buccaneers offered their captives corals, knives and axes, which they accepted; they also treated them in a very friendly manner, offering them food and drink, but this they would not touch. All the time they were prisoners, no one saw the islanders speak a word to each other.

When they saw how afraid the Indians were of them, the buccaneers let them go, giving them a few knick-knacks to entice them, upon which they indicated that they would come back again. But they did not return, nor from then on were they ever seen on the island. No vessels were ever found in which they might have sailed away, so the buccaneers could only conclude that they must have swum across to the small islands by night.

Meanwhile, l'Olonnais and his men had been busy breaking up the great ship. Realizing it would be a considerable time before they would be able to leave, they set about cultivating the ground and planting some food-crops. First they sowed beans, and within six weeks they also had plenty of maize. With these crops, together with bananas and plantains, they were in no danger of perishing from hunger.

After living there five or six months they had built a long-boat out of the timbers of the great ship. They decided to send out an expedition along the river Nicaragua to try to capture some canoes in which to fetch off the rest of the men for whom there was no room on board. So there would be no disagreement, they drew lots to decide who should go off in the longboat and the few canoes they already had. Then half the men set off in the boats, and the other half stayed on the island.

After a few days' sailing, l'Olonnais came to the mouth of the river Nicaragua. Here the ill-luck which had been dogging his steps for some time finally caught up with him. He was set upon both by the Indians and the Spaniards: many of his men were killed and l'Olonnais and the rest were forced to flee. L'Olonnais determined not to return to his comrades on the island without a ship. He held council with the men still in his company and they resolved to take the longboat along the coast of Cartagena in an attempt to capture some vessel or other.

But now it seems God would permit this man no further wicked deeds, but was ready to punish him for all the cruelties he had inflicted on so many innocent people by a cruel death. On arrival in the Gulf of Darien, he and his men fell into the hands of those savages the Spaniards called Indios Bravos. According to one of his companions, who only saved himself from a like fate by running away, l'Olonnais was hacked to pieces and roasted limb by limb. This was the end of a man who had spilt so much guiltless blood and committed so many grisly atrocities.

The other men who had stayed on the island, having received no news of l'Olonnais, managed to embark on a buccaneer ship come from Jamaica with the intention of landing at Cabo Gracias a Dios, going upriver in canoes and taking the city of Cartagena. The two bands of buccaneers were very pleased to have encountered each other – the one at being freed from the wretched life they'd been leading for the past ten months, and the other at gaining reinforcements for carrying out their plans.

When they arrived at Cabo Gracias a Dios, the buccaneers embarked in their canoes to go upriver, leaving their ships in the river mouth, with five or six men on board each vessel. Altogether, the raiders were about 500 strong. They had brought no provisions with them, thinking to find enough on the way. This proved a mistake, for the Indians with plantations along the riverside had fled, leaving nothing behind. What little they had, the fugitives had taken into the forest with them, to live on while in hiding.

The buccaneers had not travelled far from the shore before they began to suffer great hunger, though they fed on the hope of good booty, making do meanwhile with eating any fruit they found along the river bank. But after fourteen days of travel they began to become faint from lack of proper food, so they decided to leave the river and go through the woods looking for any village or town where they might get something to eat.

But, after wandering about through the forest for several days, they were compelled to turn back without success. When they reached the river they decided to return to the coast, as many of them were dying with hunger. Indeed, they ate everything they could find – including the shoes off their feet and the sheaths of their knives. They were in such dire need they were determined to eat the Indians, if they ever met with any. But when they came among the Indians by the sea-shore, they found enough ordinary food to satisfy their hunger.

Thus ended the deeds and cruelties of François l'Olonnais and his crew. Now we shall describe the most celebrated exploits of Henry Morgan, Englishman – a man as merciless to the Spaniards as l'Olonnais had been, but more successful in his enterprises.

CHAPTER FOUR

The first exploits of Henry Morgan.

HENRY MORGAN was born in that part of Wales known as Welsh England. His father was a well-to-do farmer, but Morgan, having no liking for farm work, decided to go to sea. He reached a port where ships leave for Barbados and signed on for the voyage. On arrival, he was sold as an indentured servant in the English manner. Having served his time he went to Jamaica, where he found several buccaneer ships ready to put to sea. He joined the expedition and soon learned their manner of life. After making three or four voyages with the buccaneers, he and his comrades had made enough money out of loot and dicing to buy a ship of their own. Morgan was made captain, and they went marauding along the coast of Campeche, where they captured several ships.

At this time there was in Jamaica an old buccaneer called Mansveldt [Captain Edward Mansfield] who planned to get a fleet together to raid the mainland. Seeing that Morgan was a young man with plenty of courage, the old buccaneer invited him to join the expedition and made him vice-admiral of his fleet. When the fleet put to sea, it consisted of fifteen vessels, with 500 men, including Walloons and Frenchmen, on board.

Their first landing was on the island of St Catalina [or Providence Island] lying off the mainland coast of Costa Rica, latitude $12\frac{1}{2}°$ north, and some thirty-five leagues from the river Chagre. The buccaneers forced the Spanish garrison on the island to surrender all the fortifications. Some of these Mansveldt ordered to be demolished, and others to be reinforced. Here he left a garrison of 100 men, together with all the slaves who had belonged to the Spaniards. All the rest of the artillery was carried over to an off-shore islet, so close to St Catalina the distance could be spanned by a bridge. When all these defences had been put in good order, Mansveldt burned down all the houses on the larger island and then put to sea, taking all the Spanish prisoners with him.

After putting all these prisoners ashore near a place called Porto Bello on the mainland, the buccaneers cruised along the coast of Costa Rica. Soon they landed by the river Colla, intending to plunder all the villages and proceed to the town of Nata [on the other side of the isthmus, in the Bay of Panama]. But the President of Panama had been warned of the coming of the buccaneers, and came to meet them with a force strong enough to compel them to retreat.

As the whole coast was now on the alert, Mansveldt realized he would derive little profit by raiding at present, so decided to return to St Catalina and see how the men he had left there were getting on. He had left a Frenchman called St Simon as governor, and this man had put everything in such good order, while Mansveldt was away, that all the fortifications had been made impregnable. Crops had been sown on the little island, so they had enough food for their needs until such time as relief supplies arrived from Jamaica.

Mansveldt was strongly inclined to hold on to St Catalina, as the island made an excellent base for the buccaneers, having a good harbour and lying conveniently near the Spanish mainland coast. He decided to return to Jamaica and send back reinforcements to enable the garrison to defend the island in case of an invasion by Spanish forces from the mainland. On arrival in Jamaica, he explained to the governor his intention of holding the island of St Catalina. But the governor refused to give Mansveldt assistance. On the one hand, he feared he might incur the displeasure of the King if complaints reached the English court, and on the other that he might weaken and render ineffective the defences of Jamaica itself.

Seeing there was no help to be got in this quarter for maintaining the island, and as he had no means of achieving his objective on his own, Mansveldt decided to go to Tortuga and ask the governor for assistance. But he did not put this intention into effect, being prevented by death.

St Simon, who had been left as governor of the island, began to be anxious for news of Mansveldt. In the meantime, Don Juan Perez de Guzman, the head of government in Costa Rica and a most vigilant and intelligent soldier, realized that now was the time to recapture St Catalina, before the buccaneers received reinforcements. He equipped a considerable force which he despatched to retake the island and establish a suitable garrison there. He also sent a letter to the governor of the buccaneers, in which he promised him certain compensation if he would surrender the island willingly. St Simon saw no chance of making profitable use of the island without reinforcements, so he agreed to the Spanish terms and gave up the island.

Some days after St Catalina had been given over to the Spaniards, an English vessel, which the governor had sent on the sly, arrived from Jamaica, containing fourteen men and a few women. The Spaniards ran up the English flag, and made St Simon go down to the shore to guide the vessel into harbour. The little ship was captured and everyone on board made prisoner.

The Spaniards lit bonfires to celebrate this great victory of wresting the island from the English buccaneers. A Spanish engineer wrote an account of these events, which came into my possession, written by his own hand in the Spanish tongue. This I have translated for the satisfaction of the curious reader. The manuscript reads as follows:

A pertinent account of the fortunate victory against the English corsairs by the arms of His Catholic Majesty under the direction of Don Juan Perez de Guzman, Knight of the Order of Santiago, Governor and Captain General of the realm of Tierra Firma and the province of Veragua.

The realm of Tierra Firma, finding itself ready and able to resist the corsairs of Jamaica, received news that fourteen of their ships were cruising along the coast with intention to rob and plunder the subjects of His Catholic Majesty. On 14 June 1665, tidings came to Panama that the English pirates had come to Puerto de Naos where they had set the garrison of St Catalina on shore, including the governor, Don Esteban del Campo, from whom they had seized the island, together with 200 men of various nationalities. Upon this news, the governor and captain-general, Field Marshal Don Juan Perez de Guzman, ordered that the former prisoners be brought to the city of Porto Bello, where they gave a detailed account to His Excellency. They stated that on 27 May, about midnight, the corsairs had landed unseen, and at six o'clock next morning had possessed themselves of the fortifications, without any struggle, and had taken the people prisoner.

On 27 June His Excellency called a council of war, in which he drew attention to the great advances made daily by the pirates, saying they would make themselves masters of the West Indies, to the great disgrace and injury of the Spanish nation. Now they had the island of St Catalina under their dominion, they would under-take still more enterprises, as had already been shown by their various raids on the mainland coast. It was essential, while the corsairs were still not yet established in full strength, that forces should be sent to recapture this island.

Nevertheless, a few members of the Council did not agree, saying it was not worth the trouble, as the pirates would not find enough there to subsist on, and would be obliged to abandon the island of their own accord. The others thought the governor's proposals essential for the well-being and reputation of the Spanish crown.

His Excellency, as a courageous and wise leader, rapidly gave orders that provisions should be sent to Porto Bello for the soldiers. Not being willing to entrust the matter to anyone else, His Excellency personally supervised the expedition, disregarding the difficulties of the way, swimming across rivers – not without peril to his life, which he hazarded as a loyal subject of the King.

He arrived at Porto Bello on 7 July and, finding in harbour the *St Vicente*, a ship of the Company of Negroes, well provided with munitions of war, chartered this vessel for the expedition. He in-stalled as commandant the town-major of Porto Bello, Captain Jose Sanchez Ximenez, a brave soldier, and gave him 227 men. Forty-seven of those previously taken prisoner on St Catalina joined the expedition, going back like lions to regain their honour and show they were valiant soldiers. There were also thirty-four Spaniards from the garrison; twenty-nine half-breeds or mulattoes; twelve Indians – very skilful at shooting arrows; seven expert gunners; two adjutants; two pilots; one surgeon; and a monk of the Order Scoraphica to confess them.

Don Juan then gave instructions to the commandant, telling him that, should the governor of Cartagena not instantly assist him with men and ships as required, he was to present him with a Requisition in the name of His Majesty. The commandant, having a sufficient force of brave soldiers for the enterprise, was then to proceed to St Catalina and set about the recapture of the island. Don Juan gave him letters-of-credit on the richest merchants of Cartagena, and had the ship equipped with extra munitions of war. Then Don Juan mustered the troops, and the embarkation began.

On the fourteenth of the same month, His Excellency went on board to see the ship out of harbour, and, the wind being fair, he had the men assembled. He made them an encouraging speech, reminding them they were bound to uphold the holy Catholic faith, and punish the heretics for their audacity in plundering the churches. These men, it seemed, did not fear the arms of His Majesty's forces, since they had the boldness to occupy his territories – a thing which Don Juan, so long as he was governor, would not suffer. On the expedition's victorious return he would recompense all those who had satisfactorily done their bounden duty. With these counsels, full of a burning enthusiasm which penetrated every heart, he left the ship, which at once set sail.

The vessel arrived at Cartagena on 22 July, where the commandant, as ordered, handed over his instructions to the governor. The governor, on seeing these bold plans, decided to help him with a frigate, a galliot and three barques, together with 126 men, consisting of sixty-six Spaniards and sixty mulattoes. Don Jose Ramirez de Leyba was their captain, the whole fleet being under the command of the Major of Porto Bello. Being well provided with all things needful, the expedition sailed from Cartagena on 2 August.

On 10 August they sighted St Catalina, and, despite a contrary wind, came to anchor in the port, having lost one barque on the reef of Quita Siños in a storm.

The enemy fired three volleys of ball cartridges, which instantly received three volleys in response. The Major sent one of his officers on shore to summon the pirates to surrender the island, which they had occupied contrary to the articles of peace between the crowns of England and Spain, saying that, should they prove intransigent, they should all be put to the sword. To which they replied that the island had formerly belonged to the English crown,* and they would rather die than give it up again now.

On Friday, 13 August, three Negroes deserted from the enemy and came on board the admiral's ship, stating that the defenders were no more than seventy-two strong, and full of fear on seeing such a powerful invading force. Upon this news, trusting in victory and being well prepared, we advanced closer to the fort, which kept up a heavy cannonade until darkness fell.

On Sunday, 17 August, the feast of the Assumption of Our Lady, the weather being quite calm, our men prepared to land, and the victorious battle was fought as follows.

The admiral's ship, the *St Vicente*, kept up a heavy fire all day on the battery known as la Concepcion. The vice-admiral, the *St Pedrito*, together with the galliot, fired on the St Jago battery.

The sloops brought the men on shore near this battery, from which they marched towards the position known as Cortadura. Francisco Carceres, the adjutant, led his fifteen men to reconnoitre the enemy strength, but had to retire on reaching the Cortadura fort, the enemy firing off batteries of sixty muskets fastened like organ pipes and fired simultaneously. Captain Don Jose Ramirez de Leyba advanced with sixty men to attack the Cortadura fort, which they conquered after a very hard battle.

Captain Juan Galeno, with a contingent of ninety men, including half-breeds and Indians, and the three blacks who had defected from the enemy, crossed over the hills to attack the fort of St Teresa. Major Don Jose Sanchez Ximenez, as commander-in-chief, having assaulted the battery of St Jago, crossed the harbour with the rest of the troops in four sloops, and effected a landing in despite of the enemy's heavy fire with cannon and muskets. At the

* *Translator's note:* St Catalina, or Providence, had been garrisoned by the Spanish since 1641. On its capture in that year, the English settlers had to forfeit their property and leave the island on pain of death.

same time Captain Juan Galeno began to storm the fort of St Teresa, so that our men were assaulting the enemy in three places simultaneously, with such courage that six of the enemy were killed.

The enemy, seeing they could hold out no longer, took flight and shut themselves in the Cortadura fort, whence they cried for quarter. Their lives being granted them, they immediately surrendered all the fortifications. Presently Don Jose Ramirez came marching over the bridge, and the whole island was at once surrendered to him, and the flag was hoisted in the name of His Majesty. Prayers of thanks were also made to the Divine Majesty, who had been pleased to grant such a great and happy victory on the feast of the Assumption of the Blessed Virgin.

The number of English dead was six, and several wounded, together with seventy prisoners; our own casualties were one dead and four wounded. On the island were found 2,800 pounds of gunpowder, 250 pounds of musket bullets, 800 pounds of fuse and various other munitions of war. The following day the Major (as was his bounden duty) had two Spaniards shot dead for supporting the English pirates and taking up arms against the King.

On 10 September an English ship was sighted, and the governor ordered M. St Simon, a Frenchman by birth, to say the island was still in English hands, which he promptly obeyed. When the small ship entered harbour it was found to contain fourteen men, a woman and her daughter. These sixteen persons were placed with the other prisoners.

These English pirates were taken back to the mainland, where His Excellency ordered that three of them should be taken to Panama, and the rest should stay in Porto Bello, to work there in the fort of St Jerome. This is a square fortification of the strongest possible construction, made of lime and stone, conveniently situated in the middle of the port. It stands eighty-eight feet high, with walls fourteen feet thick; its ramparts extend seventy-five feet in diameter, making a total diameter of 300 feet with the storehouses and all the works inside included. This castle has been built without expense to His Majesty, a great sum having been contributed by His Excellency himself . . . etc.

I have given a word for word translation of this account, so that the reader may see what a great outcry the Spaniards make of a business of little importance, and what a performance they made to oust seventy men from an island they were quite willing to leave. Notwithstanding the might of the Spaniards, if the buccaneers had wished to hold the island they could easily have driven them off.*

* *Translator's note:* This final derisory paragraph is omitted in the English translation of 1684, which was based on the Spanish translation of Exquemelin's work.

CHAPTER FIVE

Morgan attempts to keep St Catalina as a strong-hold for the buccaneers, but fails. A description of Cuba. The invasion and capture of Puerto del Principe.

ON the death of Mansveldt, his old admiral, Morgan himself would gladly have kept St Catalina as a robbers' eyrie, having used the island on various occasions as a rendezvous with his comrades. He was constantly looking for means of putting this plan into effect, and had written to various merchants in New England to send out supplies to the island. In time, he intended to have made St Catalina so strong it would have been impossible for the Spaniards to oust him, nor would the might of the King of England have been able to do much damage to his position. His schemes came to nothing, however, when the island was lost to the Spaniards.

Morgan refused to be daunted, but on the contrary began setting new plans afoot. He equipped a ship, resolving to make up a fleet of as many buccaneers as he could bring together in order to launch an attack on some important city in the Spanish dominions. He gave his fellow rovers a rendezvous in the South Cays of Cuba, where the fleet could assemble and at once consider where to attack. So that my readers may fully understand this account, I shall first give a brief description of the island.

Cuba lies between latitudes 20 and 23° north, extending 160 leagues from east to west, and forty leagues in width. It is no less fruitful than Hispaniola, and exports an immense quantity of hides, known in Europe as Havana hides. Cuba is surrounded by innumerable small islands, known as Cays, frequently used by the buccaneers as bases from which to harry the Spaniards.

The island has several fine rivers and some excellent ports. In the south are St Jago, St Maria, Espiritu Santo, Trinidad, Xagua, Cabo de Corrientes and more besides, while on the north side lie Havana, Puerto Mariano, Santa Cruz, Mataricos, Puerto del Principe and Baracao. St Jago is the capital of half the island, and has a resident governor and a bishop. Most of its commerce is with the Canary Islands, where it sends sugar, tobacco and hides from its subordinate towns. Although protected by a fort, this city has been plundered by buccaneers from Jamaica and Tortuga.

Havana, the capital of the western part of the island, is one of the strongest and most famous cities in all the West Indies. Its major export is excellent tobacco, with which it supplies all New Spain and Costa Rica, as far as the South Sea. Havana is defended by three strong forts – two in the port, and one on a hill commanding the town. There are more than 10,000 inhabitants, the merchants trading with New Spain, Campeche, Honduras and Florida. All the ships from New Spain, Caracas, Cartagena, Costa Rica and Honduras call in there to take on fresh supplies on their way to Spain, since it lies on their route. The silver fleet always calls in there, to complete its cargo with hides and logwood.

Morgan had hardly been two months in the South Cays of Cuba before he had assembled a fleet of some twelve vessels, with 700 men, both English and French. He called a general council to decide where they should attack. Some proposed a surprise assault by night on Havana itself, saying they could easily plunder the city and carry off some of the priests as prisoner before the forts were ready to put up any defence. Everyone gave his opinion on this proposal, but it was not carried. Some of the men had been prisoners in Havana, and they declared the buccaneers were not yet strong enough to plunder the city. If they could form a fleet of 1,500 men, then there would be a good chance of taking Havana. In that case, the ships could be anchored off the Island of Pines and the men sent upriver in small boats to Matamano, only fourteen leagues from Havana. However, as the buccaneers had no means of getting together such a force, they resolved to attack elsewhere.

Another man proposed an assault on Puerto del Principe. He had been there, he said, and there was plenty of money in the town, for it was where the Havana merchants came to buy hides. Lying at some distance from the sea, the place had never been plundered, so the inhabitants had no fear of the English.

This proposal was considered and agreed upon, and Morgan at once ordered his fleet to weigh anchor and set sail for the port of St Maria, the nearest place to Puerto del Principe. Before they reached this destination a Spaniard, who had long been a prisoner in the hands of the English and had picked up some words of their language, overheard the buccaneers muttering about Puerto del Principe. This man jumped overboard one night and began swimming for the nearest island. The English at once sprang into their canoes to fish him out again, but he managed to land before they could catch him and hid among the trees, where they could not find him.

Next day this Spaniard swam from one islet to the next till he reached the Cuban coast. He was familiar with the roads and before long arrived at Puerto del Principe, where he warned the inhabitants of the corsairs' approach and the forces at their disposal. The Spaniards immediately began hiding their goods, while the governor assembled all the men he could, including a number of slaves. He had a great number of trees felled to block the road and laid various ambushes, mounted with cannon. About 800 men were mustered, both from the town itself and from neighbouring places. Having manned the ambuscades with as many as he judged necessary, the governor kept the main body of defenders in an open field near the city, whence he could see the enemy's approach from afar.

The Spaniards were still busy equipping their ambuscades when the buccaneers came upon them unawares. Finding the road blocked, they had made their way through the woods, thus avoiding several of the traps set for them. At length they reached the open field, or savana as the Spanish call it. The governor, thinking the enemy would be full of fear when they saw the numerous forces he had gathered to resist them, instantly despatched a troop of horsemen to take them from the rear and cut them down as they fled. But events fell out otherwise.

The buccaneers, who had been advancing all this time with drums beating and banners flying, now began to spread out in a half-moon and at the same time to fall upon the Spaniards, who at first resisted them fiercely – but the battle did not last for long. The buccaneers never missed their mark, and kept up a continuous fire without pausing in their charge. The defenders' courage began to flag, especially when they saw their governor fall. They began to retreat towards the forest, where they would have a better chance of escape, but most of them were struck down before they reached shelter, although some finally did escape in the woods.

The buccaneers now made their way towards the town, victors of the field and full of high spirits, for although the battle on the savana had lasted four hours, they had suffered few casualties. Soon they entered the town, where they encountered fresh resistance from a group who had stayed there with the women, helped by some who had taken part in the battle on the savana and still hoped to prevent the enemy from plundering the town. Some locked themselves in their houses and fired from the windows, but once the buccaneers became aware of this sniping they threatened to burn down the whole town, destroying women and children and all. The Spaniards then surrendered, fearing these menaces would be put into effect, and believing the rovers would be unable to hold the town under subjection for long.

The buccaneers shut up the Spaniards, including women and children and slaves, in the church, and collected all the loot they could find in the town. When this was done, they began to go out on marauding expeditions, every day bringing back fresh booty and prisoners, so time did not lie heavy on their hands. In fact, they led a life after their own hearts, eating and drinking so long as there was anything to find. But time did not pass so lightly for the poor wretched prisoners in the church, living in fear. They were given little to eat, and every day were pained and plagued by unspeakable tortures to make them say where they had hidden money or goods. Many a poor man was tortured who had neither, who earned only enough by his daily labour to support his wife and family. It made no difference to these tyrants, who said, 'If he won't confess, string him up.' There were poor women with babies at their breast and no nourishment to give these innocents, for the mothers themselves were dying of hunger and discomfort, but neither did their plight rouse any compassion in the buccaneers. When they felt like it, they would shoot a cow or bull and, having helped themselves to the best meat, would give the remains to the prisoners, who could do what they pleased with it.

But when there was nothing more to eat or to drink or to plunder, the buccaneers decided to take their leave. They informed the prisoners that money must be found for their ransom or otherwise they would be transported to Jamaica, and also that they must pay a ransom for the city, or the rovers would burn it to ashes before they left. They sent out four of the Spanish prisoners to collect this tribute, and to speed up the payment subjected the rest to further torments.

The four Spaniards returned, and went lamenting to Morgan, the general of the buccaneers, saying they had done their best to get hold of ransom money but they had been unable to find any of the people in hiding. If he would only wait another fortnight, they were sure the money he demanded could be collected. While they were busy negotiating with Morgan about the ransom, seven or eight buccaneers, who had been out of town shooting cattle, returned with a Negro prisoner. This man had been carrying letters meant for some of the prisoners. These were opened, and proved to be from the governor of St Jago, saying he would soon be coming to relieve the town, and telling them not to be too hasty in paying any ransom or levy. They must delay matters for another fortnight if possible, giving the buccaneers hope that the money would then be paid.

Seeing the Spaniards intended to play him false, Morgan had all the plunder instantly carried to the shore where his ships lay, and announced that unless the ransom was paid next day he would set the town on fire. He said nothing about the letters which had come into his hands. The Spaniards again answered that it was impossible: their people were scattered here and there, and the money could not be collected in so short a time. Morgan, well aware of their secrets, then said they must send 500 cattle to the sea-shore, together with salt to preserve the meat. They agreed to this arrangement, and Morgan and the buccaneers marched down to the shore, taking six of the principal citizens as hostages, together with all the captured slaves.

Next morning the Spaniards brought the 500 beasts they had promised down to the shore where the fleet lay anchored, and asked for their hostages back again. But Morgan, who did not trust them and had no desire to fight when there was no booty to be gained from it, refused to give up his prisoners before all the meat was on board. The Spaniards, in order to release their fellow-citizens and leaders with all speed, helped the buccaneers to slaughter the animals and salt the flesh. The buccaneers gladly let them do this work, which left them with scarcely anything to do but carry the meat on board.

In the meantime, trouble broke out between the French and the English because an Englishman had shot a Frenchman dead on account of a marrow-bone. I have recounted earlier how the *boucaniers*, when they have killed a beast, suck out the marrow, and these men did the same thing. The Frenchman had flayed an animal and the Englishman came up and helped himself to the marrow-bones. This started the quarrel, and they challenged each other to fight it out with muskets. On coming to the duelling place, away from the rest, the Englishman was ready before the other, and shot him through the body from behind. Upon this, the French seized their muskets and wanted to fall on the English, but Morgan thrust himself between the rival groups and promised the French he would do right by them and have the Englishman hanged as soon as they reached Jamaica.

The man would have had no blame if he had not shot his opponent treacherously, for duels are a daily occurrence among the buccaneers – but they have to be fought fairly. When a man kills his opponent in fair fight, no more questions are asked. Morgan had the criminal bound hand and foot, to take him along to Jamaica.

Meanwhile the meat had been salted and loaded in the ships, and then Morgan handed over the hostages and his fleet set sail. He had given each ship a rendezvous on one of the islands, where they could share out the spoils. On arrival, they found this amounted to some 50,000 pieces of eight in ready money, silverwork and the various other goods they had pillaged. They had hoped for greater booty: this amount was of little help to them, for it would not even pay the debts they owed in Jamaica.

Morgan proposed going to plunder some other place before returning to Jamaica, but the French could not agree with the English and went their own way, leaving Morgan with only his own people. He had pointed out to the French that he would have been very glad of their company, and had promised to give them protection, but they did not wish to stay. Nevertheless, they parted good friends, and Morgan promised he would have justice done on behalf of their comrade who had been shot. This he did, for as soon as he arrived at Jamaica he had the treacherous duellist instantly hanged.

CHAPTER SIX

*Morgan decides to attack Porto Bello, equips
his fleet, and conquers the city with a small force.*

AFTER the French had separated from Morgan, it seemed the
English had not so much heart for attacking another place,
since their numbers were so depleted. But Morgan put spirit
into them, saying he knew ways of making them rich if only
they would follow him. The high hopes Morgan held out
made them agree. He was joined by another buccaneer ship
which had been in Campeche, so now he was admiral of a fleet
of nine vessels, with a strength of 460 men. When all was
finally ready, he put to sea without revealing his plans, his
men being sustained only by the prospect of rich booty. He
set his course towards the mainland coast, the fleet coming in
sight of Costa Rica after a few days.

At this point Morgan revealed his intention to his captains,
and afterwards to the crews: this was to assault Porto Bello
by night and pillage the city. The raid would be easy to accom-
plish, he argued, as no one was aware of their presence on the
coast. Some replied that they were but few for such an undertaking – upon which Morgan said if they were few in number
each man's portion would be so much the greater. The resolution was agreed, and forth they went.

So that the reader may better understand this audacious
exploit, I must give a short description of Porto Bello. This
city is in Costa Rica [in Panama, actually] latitude 10° north,
some forty leagues from the Gulf of Darien and eight leagues
west of Nombre de Dios. With the exception of Havana and
Cartagena, it is the strongest city which the King of Spain
possesses in all the West Indies. Two strong forts stand at the
entrance of the bay, protecting the town and harbour. These
forts are always manned by a garrison of 300 soldiers, and not

a single vessel can enter the bay without consent. Four hundred families have their permanent residence in the city, but the merchants only stay there when there are galleons in port, as the place is very unhealthy on account of the mountain vapours. The merchants reside in Panama, but have their warehouses in Porto Bello, kept up by their servants. Silver is brought from Panama on pack-mules, ready for the arrival of the galleons, or the ships of the slave trade, delivering Negroes.

Morgan, who was very familiar with this coast, arrived with his fleet about dusk off Puerto de Naos, some ten leagues west of Porto Bello, and crept along the coast by night until they reached Puerto del Pontin, four leagues from the city. There they cast anchor, and the buccaneers all jumped into canoes and small rowing-boats, leaving just enough men on board to manage the ships and bring them into port next day.

About midnight they landed at a place called Estero Longa Lemo, and marched overland until they reached the first outpost of the city. Their guide was an Englishman who had formerly been a prisoner there and so knew the roads well. This Englishman and three or four others went ahead and captured the sentry, without firing a shot or making any noise. They bound him fast and brought him to Morgan, who immediately questioned him as to the arrangements of the town's defences and the strength of the garrison, and the prisoner told what he knew. Still with his hands tied, they made him march in the vanguard, threatening that if he had not told them the truth it would cost him his life.

After marching about a quarter of an hour they came to a redoubt, which they surrounded. Morgan called on the defenders to surrender, or else they would receive no quarter. Despite this threat the defenders proved stubborn and bravely fired on their attackers, so that at least they could give warning to the people in the city. In fact, the alarm was immediately sounded there. But the redoubt could not hold out long, and as soon as the buccaneers entered they blew up the inner fortification with all the Spaniards inside.

Then the buccaneers rushed on to the city, where most of the people were still in bed – for no one had thought the corsairs would have been so bold as to attack a place like Porto Bello. As the rovers entered, those citizens who were up grabbed what they had and flung it down cisterns and wells, hoping to foil the invaders. One band of buccaneers went to assault the forts and another went to the cloisters, where they took all the monks and nuns prisoner.

The governor had retired to one of the forts, from which he directed a fierce fire against the buccaneers, who were not slow to answer him. They kept up such a steady aim on the gun-platforms that the Spaniards lost seven or eight men before they could load and fire. The battle lasted all morning till noon, and still the invaders could not conquer the fort. Their ships lay in the harbour-mouth, and no one could enter for the withering fire from the forts on both sides. Finally, as they had lost many men and were gaining no advantage, the buccaneers began throwing in hand grenades and endeavoured to burn down the gate of the fort. But when they came in close for this attack the Spaniards soon made them turn back, for they hurled down at least fifty pots full of gunpowder as well as huge stones, which did much damage among the raiders.

Morgan and his men were beginning to despair, when they saw the English flag flying from the smaller fort and a troop of their fellows approaching, shouting 'Victory!' This sight made Morgan pluck up courage, despite the drubbing he'd had. He entered the town to think of some means of capturing the fort, which was a matter of great importance to the buccaneers as the principal citizens were inside, with their gold and silver and jewels, and the silver ornaments from the churches.

Morgan had a dozen huge ladders made, broad enough for four men to climb at the same time. He fetched out all the monks and nuns, and the governor was informed that unless he surrendered the fort these people would be made to set the scaling ladders against its walls. All the answer Morgan received was that he should never have the fort so long as the governor lived.

The ladders were brought out, carried by the monks, priests and women, urged on by the buccaneers, who never thought the governor would fire on his own people – but he spared them as little as he had the raiders. The monks began to implore the governor by all the saints in heaven to give up the fort and save their lives, but their cries went unheeded. Willing or not, they had no choice but to carry out the ladders. As soon as these were set against the walls the buccaneers immediately swarmed up, furiously attacking the Spaniards with hand grenades and stink-pots – but they were forced to turn back by the ferocious resistance of the defenders.

The buccaneers refused to be daunted. One troop managed to set the fort gate on fire, while the rest clambered up the ladders with the same violence as before. When the Spaniards saw they were attacking with such vehemence, they gave up the defence – all except the governor, who like a desperate madman slew his own folk as well as the enemy. The buccaneers demanded if he would accept quarter, and he answered no. He used these very words: '*Más vale morir como soldado honrado que ser ahorcado como un cobardo.*' ('Better to die as an honourable soldier than be hanged as a coward.') They attempted to take him prisoner but could not, and were forced to shoot him dead. His own wife and daughter, who were in the fort with him, had begged him to save his life, but to no avail.

After the surrender of the fort, which was in the evening, all the prisoners were brought inside the town, the men and women being housed separately, and a guard set to look after them. The rovers brought their own wounded into a house near by. Having put everything in order, they began making merry, lording it with wine and women. If fifty stout-hearted men had been at hand that night they could have wiped out all the buccaneers.

Next day the rovers began collecting the loot, searching all the houses. Some of the prisoners were made to point out who were the richest among them, and then these citizens were asked where their wealth was. If they refused to tell they were immediately put to the rack and tortured there until they gave up the ghost or confessed the hiding-place. Many innocent souls, who in fact had nothing to hide, died like martyrs under the torments their captors subjected them to. No one was spared, except those who revealed where their goods were hidden.

Meanwhile, the president of Panama, having received news of the conquest of Porto Bello, was busy gathering together a force sufficient to drive the corsairs out of that city. The buccaneers were warned of this activity by some prisoners they had taken, but they paid little attention to the news. Their ships lay in the harbour, and if they could no longer hold the town they would set it on fire and put to sea.

When they had been there a fortnight diseases began to rage among them, caused by air foul with the stench of so many corpses, and by their furious debaucheries with drink and women. Most of their wounded died. As for the Spanish, very few survived – but these did not die from excesses, but through want and discomfort. Instead of sipping their customary morning cup of chocolate, they were glad to get a bit of bread or a lump of mule's flesh.

Meantime, Morgan was getting everything ready for their departure. The booty was stowed on board, together with as much foodstuff as they could obtain. Morgan informed the prisoners he must have a ransom for the city, otherwise he would set it on fire and demolish the forts. So that they could attend to this matter, he gave them permission to send out two men to collect the levy, which amounted to 100,000 pieces of eight. The two men sent to fetch this contribution went to the president of Panama and told him what was happening in Porto Bello.

The president had already raised a considerable army, and now led these troops to Porto Bello. The buccaneers, who were on the alert, were warned of his advance and lay in wait for him with 100 well-armed men at a narrow passage. They succeeded in destroying many of the president's troops and then retired to the fort. The president then sent word to Morgan that unless the buccaneers moved out he would attack with a huge army and grant no quarter whatsoever. Morgan was not afraid, knowing he could get away whenever he chose, and answered that he would not abandon the forts until the demanded ransom was produced. And, in the extreme event of his having to leave, he would at least demolish the forts beforehand and put all his prisoners to death.

Seeing no means of coercing the buccaneers, the president left the citizens of Porto Bello to manage as best they could and withdrew with his troops from the city. In the end, the citizens contrived to collect the 100,000 pieces of eight to secure their liberty.

The president of Panama was astounded that 400 men could have conquered such strong fortresses, whose defenders had not lacked courage, with nothing but small-arms. He sent a messenger to Morgan, asking that he might be allowed to see the weapon which had given him such power. Morgan received the president's envoy with great civility and gave him a French musket with a barrel four and a half feet long, firing a one ounce bullet; he also sent a cartouche which he'd had expressly made in France, containing thirty cartridges full of powder. He charged the messenger to tell his master that Morgan presented him with this musket, and that within a year or two he would come to Panama to fetch it back again.

The president sent the messenger back with a present for Morgan – a gold ring set with a rosette of emeralds – and thanked him cordially for the musket. He begged Morgan not to call on him in the manner he had visited Porto Bello, for in that case he might not get such a good reception.

Morgan, having stocked his ships with all kinds of provisions and marine stores, of which there were plenty in Porto Bello, finally took his departure. He could not resist taking some of the brass cannon from the forts as a keepsake, and the rest of the guns were spiked.

Shortly after abandoning Porto Bello, the fleet arrived at

the South Cays of Cuba, where, according to custom, the booty was shared out. The buccaneers found they had 215,000 pieces of eight in ready money, jewels and silver, besides other spoils of linen, silk and other goods. Having shared out the plunder, Morgan entered Jamaica with great honour and magnificence, as he brought so much wealth with him.

CHAPTER SEVEN

*The capture of the city of Maracaibo, on the coast
of New Venezuela; marauding in Lake Maracaibo and the destruction of three Spanish ships
which attempt to prevent the buccaneers' escape.*

AFTER Morgan had been some time in Jamaica and his
men had squandered their money, he decided to renew
his attacks on the Spaniards. He gave as rendezvous the Isla
de la Vaca, off the south coast of Hispaniola. This was a
good place for careening the ships and also for obtaining
provisions, as there are many wild boar to hunt on the
big island. Many English and French buccaneers arrived
to join forces with Morgan, for he had made a great name for
himself on account of the immense success of his previous
raids.

At this time a naval vessel mounting thirty-six guns arrived
in Jamaica from New England. The governor sent this warship to join Morgan's fleet, to encourage him still further to
attack some place of consequence, where there would be good
plunder. Morgan was delighted at the arrival of such a ship,
for he had not a single vessel in his fleet fit to prevail against a
fort if the need arose. There was also a French ship, mounting
twenty-four cannon and twelve brass swivel-guns, which
Morgan would gladly have had in his company. But the men
on board dared not trust themselves among the English, fearing reprisals. At a time when they had run short of food they
had encountered an English ship at sea and had helped themselves to victuals with no payment except a bill of exchange
payable in Jamaica and Tortuga.

Seeing the French would not accompany him willingly,
Morgan invited the captain and crew on board the great ship,
without rousing their suspicions, then took them all prisoner,

laying claim to the French ship on account of the victuals they had taken.

Morgan then held a council of war with the captains of the buccaneer fleet to decide which place on the Spanish coast to attack. They resolved to sail first for the island of Savona, off the eastern point of Hispaniola, and having come together at this rendezvous take a further decision as to where they would go.

They drank the health of the King of England and toasted their good success and fired off salvoes. The gentlemen made merry in the poop and the men did the same in the fo'c'sle – but when they were at the height of their joy, events swiftly changed to a sorrowful conclusion. For, as the festive guns were being fired, some sparks landed in the gunpowder – and the ship blew up with 300 Englishmen on board, as well as the French prisoners. There were only about thirty survivors. All those who had been in the great cabin saved their lives, with little harm done, Morgan being slightly injured in the leg. The survivors had all been in the stern of the ship, for in English ships the powder-room is generally forward. More might have escaped, but most of the men had been drunk.

The English, having no excuse for the disaster which had overtaken the warship, justified matters by taking the French vessel. They said the French had blown up the king's ship, and that they had been sailing with a Spanish privateering commission to attack the English wherever they could. As proof, they showed a pass from the governor of Baracao on the island of Cuba which they had found on the French ship, permitting the French to cruise against the English pirates, as the Jamaican buccaneers were daily committing hostilities against the Spaniards although there was no war between England and Spain.

In fact, the French had obtained this commission not to give them excuse for attacking the English buccaneers, but in order to trade with the Spaniards. The captain of the French ship was also among the survivors, and tried vainly to explain how matters stood. The ship was taken to Jamaica, where again the French captain tried to plead his cause – but instead of giving him a hearing, they threw him into prison and threatened to hang him.

Meanwhile, Morgan refused to lose heart, and decided to pursue his plans with the men who remained. A week after the ship had blown up, they had fished out all the corpses floating in the water. This was not in order to give them a decent burial, but for the sake of their clothes and the gold rings on their fingers. As soon as they had fished out a body they pulled off the garments and hacked off the fingers which were beringed, then threw back the corpse to be a floating prey for the sharks. Their bones are still to be found on the beaches, washed up by the sea.

Morgan kept to his original plan of meeting on Savona and there holding a council to decide where to attack. He set sail for this rendezvous with his companion ships, which numbered fifteen. Morgan sailed in the largest, which mounted only fourteen guns. Altogether, he had a force of about 960 men. A few days later they came to Cabo de Lobos, situated midway along the south coast of Hispaniola between Cabo Tiburon and Punta del Espada, where Morgan was held up for three weeks by the strong east wind. Every day they attempted to round the cape, but failed. Finally they succeeded, and seven or eight leagues farther on sighted a ship come from England. A few of the ships went off to see what they could get from this vessel, but Morgan continued his course, saying he would wait for them at the Bay of Ocoa.

Two days later Morgan reached this bay, where he put in to fetch aboard fresh water and to wait for the rest of his fleet. Every day five or six men from each ship were sent ashore to look for food to save their own supplies. They shot everything they found – horses, donkeys, cattle and sheep. The Spaniards of course did not suffer this gladly. Noticing that on each trip only a few men came ashore, they laid a trap for the rovers. They sent for three or four hundred soldiers from the nearby garrison at San Domingo, and meanwhile drove all the cattle inland.

The buccaneers, about fifty strong, had wandered three leagues or so through the woods when the Spaniards let them see a fine herd of cattle, driven along by a few cowherds for the look of the thing. The buccaneers fell on their prey and the Spaniards let them get on with it – but when they were in the act of carrying off the beasts they had shot, the soldiers attacked in full force, crying, '*Mata! Mata!*' ('Kill, kill!')

The buccaneers abandoned the slaughtered animals and put themselves in a posture of defence. They resisted the Spaniards furiously: while half were firing, the rest were loading. Keeping up a continuous fire, they retired in good order until they reached the shelter of the forest once more. The Spaniards would have liked to have pursued them, but, as the rovers seldom missed their mark and had already killed and wounded a large number, they turned back again.

The buccaneers were still in the woods, binding up their comrades' wounds as best they could, and they could see the Spaniards carrying off their dead and wounded. Among the casualties was a dead buccaneer, and a group of Spaniards were moving round this man, plunging their naked swords into the corpse and shouting, '*El cornudo ladron!*'

The buccaneers in the woods, seeing that the main Spanish force had withdrawn, rushed out on this troop, killing many of them. They took the corpse of their comrade, which had received more than a hundred stabs after death, and buried it in the forest. After this, they killed a few horses so as not to return without meat, and brought their wounded back on board.

Next day Morgan himself landed with 200 men, but by that time the Spaniards had already gone, and had driven away all their cattle. So they set fire to a few houses and returned to the ships.

As the rest of his fleet did not arrive, Morgan proceeded with those ships he had with him to the final rendezvous on Savona. There were no signs of the other vessels there, either, so he decided to wait a few days for them. In the meantime, he sent out a party of 150 men to land on Hispaniola and plunder the villages in the neighbourhood of San Domingo for supplies, as they were beginning to run short of food. But the marauding party returned without success, for the Spaniards, warned that the corsairs were on the coast, had all been up in arms. The buccaneers, who only cared to fight for booty, had not fancied doing battle.

As his companions still did not arrive, Morgan mustered the men who were with him. He found he had about 500 men, and eight vessels, his own ship being the biggest. His original plan had been to plunder all the towns and villages along the coast of Caracas, but his present forces were too weak for this, so he had to make another decision. Among his men was a French captain, who had been with l'Olonnais at the capture of Maracaibo. He had observed the features of the lake so accurately he was convinced he could bring in Morgan's fleet. After he had discussed with Morgan the way they must set about taking the place, the men were informed, and they agreed unanimously to go on this enterprise.

The resolve having been taken, Morgan and his fleet steered towards Curaçao and, on sighting this island, put in at another called Ruba, which lies about twelve leagues off the western tip of Curaçao. It belongs to the Dutch West India Company, who have installed a sergeant there as governor, with fifteen soldiers. Otherwise, the island is inhabited by Indians, who speak Spanish and are under Spanish religious influence. Every year a priest comes from a village called Coro on the opposite coast, who preaches to them and gives them the sacrament after the Roman Catholic manner.

These Indians trade with the buccaneers when they call in, exchanging sheep and goats for linen, thread and anything else they need. The island is infertile – very barren, and mostly overgrown with scrub. There are sheep and goats in great numbers and a little maize is planted. There are also many horses, and whatever the Indians do, they do on horseback – even if it's only to go five hundred paces from their home to fetch water. There are many rattlesnakes and some extremely venomous spiders. Anyone who has been bitten by one of these creatures is tied in a hammock and left there twenty-four hours without food or drink. The inhabitants believe the victim must be prevented from drinking, otherwise he will die.

Morgan, having come to anchor at this island, traded with the Indians for as many sheep and goats as were required for the whole fleet, and two days later left by night, so that they should not see in which direction he sailed – but they did notice it, nevertheless.

Next day the fleet entered the Bay of Maracaibo. They anchored in eight fathoms of water in the middle of the bay, out of view of Look-out Island, and sailed on when darkness fell. At daybreak they were at the bar of the lake. The Spaniards had built a new fort, from which they welcomed Morgan with the heavy artillery they had installed.

All the smaller boats were employed to land the buccaneers with the utmost speed. The Spaniards too were busy with their preparations at the fort. They burned down several near-by houses to give them a clear field of fire, and kept up a heavy cannonade all day long.

It was dusk when Morgan and his men reached the fort. They found nobody inside, for when they saw the buccaneers close by the walls the Spaniards had let off some gunpowder and made for the woods under cover of the smoke. Morgan was amazed to find no defenders, for the fort was very well equipped to hold out. They found a cellar full of gunpowder, much of it scattered about – and a length of burning match about an inch away from the powder, so that the buccaneers narrowly missed being blown up with the fort and all.

The match was snatched away, and Morgan had all the gunpowder instantly carried outside. The walls were pulled down where necessary, and the guns dismantled. There were sixteen cannon, firing balls of eight, twelve and twenty-four pounds, eighty muskets and other weapons besides. The cannon were thrown down from the fortress walls and the gun-carriages were burnt.

Early next morning the buccaneer fleet entered the lake,

and the powder was shared out among those vessels which
carried artillery. The cannon thrown down from the fort were
spiked, and buried in the sand. The men immediately embarked again, to sail for Maracaibo as quickly as possible, but
the water was so shallow above the bar in the mouth of the
lagoon the ships could barely pass over, and some went
aground. Yet, in order to lose no time in proceeding to the
city, the crews were immediately transferred to other vessels.

About noon next day they arrived before Maracaibo and
brought the vessels close inshore, so that the men could land
under the protection of the light artillery they carried. But all
went as easily as at the Fuerte de la Barra, for all the Spaniards
had fled to the woods, leaving the city empty apart from a
few poor cripples – who could neither flee nor had anything
to lose.

The buccaneers entered the city, and searched everywhere
to make sure there were no soldiers concealed in any of the
houses or in the woods round about the city. Finding no
danger, each ship's company took up its quarters in the
houses around the market-place. The great church was made
into a guardhouse, where a watch was kept continuously. On
the same day as they occupied the city, a party of a hundred
men was at once sent out to bring back prisoners and plunder.
They returned next evening with about fifty mules laden with
various goods, and thirty prisoners – men and women, children and slaves. The prisoners were promptly tortured in the
usual manner to make them say where the fugitive citizens
were hiding. One was strappado'd and beaten, another was
spread-eagled with burning fuses between his fingers and toes,
another had a cord twisted so tight round his head his eyes
protruded like eggs. If they still would not tell they were
put to death, when there were no further torments that could
be inflicted on them.

This went on for three weeks, and every day the buccaneers sent out a marauding party, who always brought back
plenty of loot, never returning empty-handed. After they had
taken about 100 prisoners from the most important families of

Maracaibo and had robbed them of their wealth, Morgan decided to proceed to Gibraltar.

The buccaneers instantly made all the ships ready, stowed the booty and the prisoners on board and weighed anchor. They steered for Gibraltar, making preparations for battle: every man knew what he had to do. Some of the prisoners were sent on shore in advance to command the people of Gibraltar, in Morgan's name, to surrender. Should they prove intransigent, he would give them no quarter: they would receive no better treatment from these buccaneers than they did from the French two years ago.

After a few days Morgan and his fleet sailed within sight of Gibraltar, where the Spaniards put up a bold fire with their heavy guns. Instead of making any changes on this account, the rovers plucked up their courage, saying if there was going to be a tussle, there'd be plenty of booty – and that was sugar enough to sweeten any sour sauce.

The crews landed at dawn next day. Instead of taking the main road, the Frenchman – who had been there before and knew the lie of the land – remembered another way through the woods, from which they could descend on the town from the rear. They left a few men in the road, to make the Spaniards think this would be the route they would take.

But in fact the buccaneers had no need of such precautions, for the Spaniards still vividly recalled the events of two years ago when the French were there, and would rather give up the place than lose as many lives as they had done then. They had set a few ambuscades outside the village along the way they were fleeing so that if they were overtaken they could defend their retreat. They had also spiked the guns at the fort, and carried away the gunpowder.

The buccaneers found nobody in the village but a poor ignorant simpleton. They asked him where the folks had fled. He said he did not know – he had not inquired. They asked whether he knew of any plantations; he said he must have been on twenty in his lifetime. Then they demanded whether he knew where to find the gold and silver of the churches.

Yes, he replied, and brought them to the church sacristy, saying he had seen all the gold and silver there, but he did not know where it was now. When they could get no more answers out of him, they tied him up and beat him. Then the simple fellow began to shout, 'Let me go! I will show you my house and my goods and my money!'

This made the rovers think they were dealing with a rich man, who had been pretending to be a fool. They unbound him, and he brought them to a hovel, where he had buried a few earthenware dishes, plates and other trash, together with three pieces of eight. They asked him his name. 'I am Don Sebastian Sanchez,' he said, 'brother of the governor of Maracaibo.' Then they began to torture him anew, tying him up and beating him till the blood ran down his body. He cried out that if they would let him go, he would take them to his sugar-mill, where they would find all his wealth and his slaves, but when they untied him he was unable to walk. They flung him on a horse, but in the forest he told them he had no sugar-mill, nor anything in the world, and that he lived on the charity of the hospital. This was true, as they afterwards discovered.

Again they took him and bound him, hanging stones from his neck and his feet. They burned palm leaves under his face, making it so sooty with smoke he did not look like a man, and they beat him violently. He died after half an hour of these torments. They cut the rope and dragged his body into the woods, where they left him lying. So ended this simple wretch's life, as a martyr.

The same day a gang of buccaneers brought back a poor cottager with his two daughters. Early next morning they went out with this man, who had promised to bring them where the villagers were hiding. He took them to various plantations where the people certainly had been, but the Spaniards, knowing the rovers were on the prowl, kept out of sight in the forest, making little huts of branches to protect their goods from the rain. When the poor man could find nobody, the buccaneers thought he was purposely misleading them. In their rage, they killed him, hanging him from a tree, although the poor soul earnestly begged and prayed for his life. The buccaneers then spread out to lie in wait for the villagers here and there around the plantations, where they would be obliged to come to gather food to live on.

At last they captured a slave, whom they promised to take back to Jamaica, and give him as much money as a man could carry, and Spanish clothes to wear. This prospect suited the Negro very well, and he promptly led them to the hiding-places. They let the slave kill some of the prisoners they captured so that he would not run away, and he did great havoc among the Spaniards. The rovers were out on this expedition eight days, making the prisoners march along with them, and loading the captured goods on mules. Finally they had so many prisoners it was impracticable to go farther, so they decided to return to Gibraltar, bringing with them over 250 captives.

On arrival, every prisoner was interrogated as to whether he had money hidden away, or whether he knew where other people's wealth was concealed. Those who would not confess were subjected to the cruellest tortures imaginable. Among those who suffered most heavily was an old Portuguese in his sixties, because a Negro had denounced him as being very rich. This old man was seized and asked where his money was. He swore by every oath that all the money he'd had in the world was a hundred pieces of eight, and that a young man who lived near him had taken this money and run off with it.

The rovers did not believe him, but strappado'd him so violently that his arms were pulled right out of joint. He still would not confess, so they tied long cords to his thumbs and his big toes and spreadeagled him to four stakes. Then four of them came and beat on the cords with their sticks, making his body jerk and shudder and stretching his sinews. Still not satisfied, they put a stone weighing at least two hundred-weight on his loins and lit a fire of palm leaves under him, burning his face and setting his hair alight – yet despite all these torments he would not confess to having money.

Then they took him and bound him to one of the pillars of the church, which they were using as a guardhouse, and gave him one little bit of meat a day, just enough to keep him alive. After four or five days of this suffering, he begged that some friends of his from among the prisoners might be sent to him, so that he might contrive to get money to give the rovers. After talking with his friends, he offered 500 pieces of eight. The rovers would not listen to him, but instead gave him a beating and said he must talk of thousands, not hundreds, or it would cost him his life. In the end, after he had produced all the evidence he could that he really was a poor man, who earned his bread keeping a tavern, they settled for 1,000 pieces of eight.

Yet even this man had not suffered all the torments which the buccaneers inflicted on the Spaniards to make them divulge their hidden wealth. Some they hung up by their genitals, till the weight of their bodies tore them loose. Then they would give the wretches three or four stabs through the body with a cutlass, and leave them lying in that condition until God released them from their miserable plight by death. Some poor creatures lingered on for four or five days. Others they crucified, with burning fuses between their fingers and toes. Others they bound, smeared their feet with grease and stuck them in the fire.

When they had finished with the white men, the buccaneers started on the slaves. Eventually they found a slave who promised to bring them to a river which flowed into the lake, where there was a ship and four barques, laden with rich cargo, belonging to Maracaibo. Another slave was denounced as knowing the whereabouts of the governor of Gibraltar and most of the women. This man was instantly seized, but he denied it. When the rovers threatened to hang him, however, he admitted he knew and promised to lead them to the governor.

The buccaneers decided that a hundred of them should go in two small vessels to the river where the ships lay, and the rest should go and capture the governor. They set out next day, leaving the prisoners on board their ships. Morgan marched with 350 men to seek out the governor, who had retired to an island in the middle of a river, which he had fortified.

Here they arrived after marching two days. The governor's spies had warned him of their approach, so he and his people had retreated to a mountain-top, which could only be reached in single file by a narrow passage. He had also prepared some fireballs, to check the invaders should they try to climb up.

But heavy rains and the great damage the buccaneers suffered crossing a river prevented them from pressing the attack. They had lost several mules, laden with money and goods, and several women and children were drowned. Some of their weapons were unfit for use, and their powder was wet. In fact, if fifty well-armed lancers had tackled them, they could easily have killed all the buccaneers – but the Spaniards were in such a state of terror they thought the very trees in the forest as they rustled in the wind were the *ladrones*, as they called the rovers.

Finally, after many hardships, the buccaneers struggled through the water. They were able to save their own skins, but the poor women and little children fared so badly it was pitiful to see. They had to travel half a league through the forest, wading through water up to their middles. The land is very low-lying, and the rivers, swollen by the rains and the water from the mountains, had overflowed their banks.

Twelve days after their departure the rovers were back in Gibraltar bringing back a large number of prisoners, but their main attempt had miscarried. Two days later the ships returned from the river bringing the captured ship and the four barques, together with goods and prisoners. They had been unable to capture these vessels complete with their original cargo, because Spaniards in canoes had given warning of their coming. They had hurriedly unloaded most of the merchandise, intending to set fire to the vessels once they were empty. But before they could manage this, the buccaneers attacked and took the ships while there were still some goods on board, such as linen and silks.

The buccaneers had been in occupation five weeks, and had sent out various other expeditions, when they decided to leave Gibraltar. They dispatched some of their prisoners to collect a ransom for the town, threatening as usual to burn the place down if it were not forthcoming. The Spaniards returned saying they had been unable to find anybody, and that the governor had forbidden the payment of any ransom. But if Morgan would have patience, they promised to gather together 5,000 pieces of eight among themselves, and he should take hostages with him to Maracaibo until all was paid.

Morgan was anxious to leave: he had been away from Maracaibo so long and did not know how things stood there. The Spaniards had had time to assemble a big enough force to prevent his getting out of the lake. So he accepted the proposal and took four hostages. He let the prisoners go (after they had paid a ransom) but kept the slaves. They wanted to pay a ransom for the Negro who had been the rovers' guide, but Morgan would not surrender him, for without doubt the Spaniards would have burnt him alive if they could have laid hands on him.

The buccaneers weighed anchor and set sail, and four days later arrived at Maracaibo, where they found everything as they had left it. But they received news they had not expected. A poor man, who had been living at the hospital, told Morgan there were three Spanish men-of-war in the mouth of the lake, lying in wait for him, and the fort had again been well equipped with artillery and soldiers.

Morgan instantly sent out a sloop to report on these ships. The boat returned next evening, and confirmed all the old man had said. They had seen the warships and been under fire from their cannon. The warships were full of troops, and the biggest carried at least forty guns, the next thirty, and the smallest twenty-four. The fort also was well defended.

These forces were disproportionately greater than Morgan's, for his heaviest ship only carried fourteen guns. No one dared betray the fear and anxiety he felt, least of all Morgan. What were they to do? There was no exit except through the mouth of the lake where the warships lay – there was no chance of escape overland. Morgan would have preferred the warships to have sailed up to the city, rather than wait for him in the straits where their heavy guns could do him great injury. Nevertheless, it appears that God (for the punishment of the Spaniards) provided means for these raiders to save themselves from the clutches of their righteous enemies.

Morgan, to show he was not afraid, sent a Spaniard to demand ransom for the city of Maracaibo. Two days later the man came back with a letter from the Spanish admiral, which read as follows:

Letter from the Spanish general, Don Alonzo del Campo y Espinosa to Morgan, admiral of the buccaneers.

Having, through our friends and neighbours, received news that you have had the audacity to commit hostilities in the territories and cities owing obedience to His Catholic Majesty, the King of Spain my master, I have come to this place, according to my bounden duty, and have built up again that fortress which you took from a set of faint-hearts and from which you flung down the guns, that I may prevent your escape from this lake and do you all the injury my duty requires.

Nevertheless, if you will surrender with humility all which you have taken, including all the slaves and other prisoners, I will have the clemency to let you pass, that you may return to your own country. Should you obdurately resist these honourable conditions which I propose, I shall send for sloops from Caracas, in which I shall embark my troops to sail for Maracaibo, with orders to destroy you utterly and put every man to the sword. This is my final resolution: take heed, and be not ungrateful for my kindness. I have with me valiant soldiers, yearning to be allowed to revenge the unrighteous acts you have committed against the Spanish nation in America.

Signed on board His Majesty's ship, *Magdalena*, at anchor in the entry of the Lake of Maracaibo, 24 April 1669.

Don Alonzo del Campo y Espinosa.

Morgan had all the buccaneers assemble in the market-place and read out the letter, first in English and then in French. Then he asked them how they felt – would they rather surrender their booty in order to gain a free passage, or would they fight for it? The buccaneers answered with one accord that they would rather fight till the death than hand over their spoils. They'd risked their lives for it once, and were ready to do so a second time.

One of the crowd came up to Morgan and said he would undertake to destroy the great ship, with only twelve men, in the following manner. They would make a fire-ship out of the ship they had captured in the lake, fitting her out like a man-of-war, with the flag flying. On the deck would stand logs of wood with caps on top, to look like the crew, and big hollow logs (the kind called Negroes' drums) would stick out of the ports to look like guns.

This suggestion was approved, considering their dire need, yet first Morgan wanted to see if he could not get some other concession from the Spanish general. He sent back a messenger with the following proposals: that the buccaneers would leave Maracaibo without doing any harm to the city by burning or other means, and without claiming any ransom; that they would give up half of the slaves, and set free all the prisoners without ransom; and that they would refrain from exacting the contribution for Gibraltar, which had still not been paid, and would let the hostages go free.

The Spanish general replied that he refused to consider such proposals, and that if they did not surrender upon the conditions imposed by him within two days, he would destroy them by fire and sword. Upon receiving this answer, Morgan and his men instantly resolved to do everything they could to get out of the lake without surrendering their booty.

All the prisoners were shut up and closely guarded. The slaves, who had been employed fetching water and doing other jobs, were also locked up, and the buccaneers themselves did the work. They collected all the tar, pitch, brimstone and other combustibles that could be found in the city, ready to prepare the fire-ship. They filled the hold with palm leaves dipped in a mixture of pitch, tar and brimstone, covered the counterfeit cannon on deck with the same stuff and laid six pots of gunpowder under each, and sawed up half the wood-work inside the ship so that it could blow up and burn with greater force. They also made new portholes through which they stuck the long hollow logs known as Negroes' drums in place of artillery. Along the deck they set wooden props, each fitted with a cap or hat to look like a man, and then hoisted the admiral's flag.

Now the fire-ship was ready they decided to set sail for the mouth of the lake. All the prisoners were put aboard one large barque, and in another all the plunder, together with the most important women prisoners, each vessel being manned by twelve well-armed buccaneers. The barques were ordered to keep to the rear of the convoy, and at a given signal to come into the midst of the fleet as they slipped out of the trap.

The fire-ship had orders to sail on ahead, in front of the admiral's flagship, and grapple the Spanish man-of-war. If the fire-ship failed to fall foul of the Spaniard on account of the current, the admiral himself would assault the man-of-war. To mislead the enemy still further, another vessel, got up to look like a fire-ship, with kindled rope smoking on deck, was to sail behind the flagship.

After Morgan had given all these orders a general oath was taken that the buccaneers would all stand by one another to the last drop of blood. Whatever happened, they would never cry for quarter but fight to the last man. Those who behaved courageously and performed any deed of extraordinary valour, or captured a ship, should be rewarded out of the common plunder.

Upon this resolution, Morgan set sail, and on 30 April 1669, came in sight of the Spanish men-of-war, riding at anchor directly in the middle of the fairway. It was too late in the evening to go into battle, so Morgan dropped anchor about a cannon-shot from the enemy, taking the men off the fire-ship in the evening in accordance with the custom of war. All night both sides kept up a vigilant watch, and the buccaneers prepared themselves for the day to come. As soon as day began to dawn, the buccaneers were under sail with the ebb tide. The Spaniards thought the rovers had resolved to slip out with the tide; they cut their cables and got under way.

The fire-ship bore down on the Spanish man-of-war and grappled to her side. Realizing the danger, the Spanish general instantly ordered men to leap across to the fire-ship, cut down her masts and push her clear so she would drift free with the tide. Scarcely had the men jumped aboard when the deck blew up. All the combustible debris caught in the sails, setting them on fire and giving out huge flames and smoke. The general was forced to abandon ship.

The second Spanish ship, seeing their flagship on fire, was making for the shelter of the fort with all speed when she ran aground. The third ship also attempted to escape, but was too quickly pursued by one of the buccaneer fleet and soon was captured. Those of the second ship, which lay aground below the fort, knowing the buccaneers would soon assail them, took what they could out of her and set the ship on fire themselves.

The great ship drifted burning along the shore, and very few men had escaped from her. The buccaneers sailed between the shore and the ship to rescue the crew, but the Spaniards drowned rather than fall into the rovers' hands, for reasons that I shall explain later.

The buccaneers were in high spirits, having fought such a victorious battle within the space of two or three hours, and they intended to follow up their success. They all came ashore to take the fort, from which came the fierce fire of heavy artillery. The buccaneers had no other weapons but their muskets and a few hand grenades; their ships' guns were too light to breach such strong walls. All the rest of the day they engaged the fort with brisk musket-fire, and when they caught sight of any of the defenders they seldom missed their mark. But when they attempted to come in close to the wall to throw their hand grenades – then it was their turn to suffer. The Spaniards began hurling down fireballs and pots of gunpowder tied to lighted fuses with such effect the buccaneers were forced to retire, with the loss of more than thirty dead and about the same number wounded.

At dusk the buccaneers went on board again, without having achieved their objective. The Spaniards, fearing they would bring their artillery on shore, worked the whole night levelling certain mounds which might have given the enemy some advantage, and still felt confident of preventing the corsairs' escape from the lake.

The great ship had broken up about evening time and some Spaniards attempted to swim to the wreck, but were prevented by the rovers. Several prisoners had been taken, and Morgan interrogated a steersman from the small ship they had captured to find out what forces the Spaniards had had, whether reinforcements were expected, and where they would come from.

'Sir,' answered the man, in Spanish, 'I am a foreigner. Please do not harm me: I will tell you the truth of all that has occurred. We were sent out to the West Indies from Spain with six ships to cruise against the corsairs and destroy them, for the Court had received strong protests on the capture of Porto Bello. The Spanish court complained to the court of England, and the King replied that he had never given commissions for any hostility to be employed against the subjects of His Catholic Majesty. Consequently these six ships were fitted out, and sent here from Spain under the command of Don Augustin de Gusto. [Bustos?]

'His flagship was the *Nuestra Señora de la Soledad*, carrying forty-eight cannon and eighteen swivel-guns. The vice-admiral was Don Alonzo del Campo y Espinosa, commanding *La Concepcion*, mounting forty-four cannon and eighteen swivel-guns. Besides these were four other ships: *La Magdalena*, with thirty-six cannon, twelve swivels and two hundred and fifty men; the *San Luis*, with twenty-six cannon, twelve swivels and two hundred men; *La Marquesa*, with sixteen cannon, eight swivels and one hundred and fifty men; and the *Nuestra Señora del Carmen*, similarly armed and manned.

'We first arrived in Cartagena, where the two great ships were sent back to Spain, as they were too large for cruising in these waters. The four remaining vessels were sent to Campeche, under the command of Don Alonzo, to sail against the corsairs. Here we lost the *Carmen* in a storm which blew up from the north, and the three other ships sailed into harbour at San Domingo in Hispaniola. We were informed that a fleet from Jamaica had passed that way, landing a few men at a place called Alta Gracia. One of these had been taken prisoner and had stated that the rovers intended to take Caracas. Don Alonzo instantly weighed anchor and we steered for the mainland. We met a barque, which we hailed, and they told us the fleet from Jamaica – seven small ships and a boat – was in the Lake of Maracaibo.

'Upon this news we sailed here, and coming to rest before the bar fired a shot to signal for a pilot. Those on land saw we were Spanish ships and came on board. They told us the English had taken Maracaibo, and were at present in Gibraltar. Don Alonzo put heart into us for battle, and promised us all the plunder we should take from the English. He had the cannon we had salvaged from the wrecked ship carried to the fort, with two brass eighteen-pounders from his own ship.

'The pilot brought us over the bar, and Don Alonzo came ashore and rallied all the people to him, and reinforced the garrison with a hundred more men. Shortly after we received news that your people were at Maracaibo, whereupon Don Alonzo wrote you a letter. When he understood you did not intend to hand over your captures, he again roused and encouraged us, promising us the plunder. All the men then took Mass in the manner of the Roman Catholic church, and swore an oath to give no quarter nor accept quarter from the English. This is why so many drowned, for they dare not cry for mercy.

'Two days before you came upon us, a Negro informed Don Alonzo that you had made a fire-ship, but he would not believe this. He said such men did not understand how to fit up a fire-ship, and had no materials for such a purpose.'

Morgan treated this steersman well, offering him a share with the rest of the crews if he would stay with them. The man accepted, since he could do no better than stay with the rovers, and told them furthermore that there had been a good 30,000 pieces of eight on board the great ship, which was why some of the Spaniards had tried to get to the wreck. Leaving one of his ships to keep the Spaniards at bay and fish up the silver, Morgan retired with the rest of his fleet to Maracaibo. Here they repaired the captured Spanish ship, which Morgan took for his own. He sent a messenger to the general, again demanding a ransom for Maracaibo or he would burn it down.

The Spaniards, in view of the defeat they had suffered at sea, decided to pay the ransom as they could think of no other way to be rid of the rovers (although Don Alonzo would never agree to this course). They asked how much Morgan demanded and he stipulated 30,000 pieces of eight and 500 cattle to provision his ships, promising to do no damage to the city and to set the prisoners free. Finally, they settled for 20,000 pieces of eight and 500 cattle.

Next day, the Spaniards brought all the cattle and part of the money. The buccaneers slaughtered the beasts and salted the flesh, and by the time this was finished the Spaniards had brought the rest of the promised ransom. They then expected the prisoners to be released, but Morgan did not see it this way: he said he would give up the prisoners when he was out of cannon-range from the fort – hoping to get an undisputed passage for the sake of the captives.

The buccaneers weighed anchor and sailed towards the entry of the lake. The ship they had left there was awaiting them, and the crew had salvaged about 15,000 pieces of eight from the wreck of the burnt ship, together with some wrought silver and various sword-hilts and daggers, all of silver. Some of the coins had melted in the great heat and had flowed together into big lumps, weighing as much as thirty pounds.

Morgan made all the prisoners understand they must persuade the general to agree to let the buccaneers pass the fort unmolested; if he would not consent they should all be hanged from the yard-arm. The prisoners discussed what to do, and sent a messenger to Don Alonzo in the fort, beseeching him to let the rovers pass in peace, for otherwise it would cost them their lives. They sought to move him by every argument, pointing out that there were many women and little children among them, and begging him to be pleased to spare their lives.

Far from conceding, the governor returned a brusque answer, upbraiding them for cowards. If they had maintained their fort against the entrance of the corsairs as strongly as he intended to dispute their exit, the raiders would not have got in so easily. On no account was he minded either to surrender the fort or to give the pirates any loophole of escape. On the contrary, he would send the lot of them to the bottom. The fort was his, he himself had wrested it from the enemy, and therefore he could do with it whatever he thought good for the advantage of his King and the maintenance of his own honour.

The Spanish messengers returned very fearfully on board and told Morgan all Don Alonzo had said. Morgan replied that he would find a means of getting out, notwithstanding. In the meantime, he thought it best to share out the booty, for there was no convenient rendezvous near at hand. The next place was Hispaniola, and before they were able to reach that island they might be separated by a storm – in which case the ship with the plunder might perhaps not care to seek out the others to give them their share.

The money, together with the jewels and wrought silver, came to the value of 250,000 pieces of eight, apart from the other goods and the slaves. This treasure was first divided among the ships according to the number of men on board, and shared out among each crew. So that all should be uprightly done, they took an oath that no man had held back so much as six pennyworth, be it in gold, silver, jewels, pearls or precious stones such as diamonds, emeralds and bezoar-stones. Morgan himself first took the oath on the Bible, and all the rest followed suit, down to the last man.

Having shared out all the booty, the buccaneers had to seek a way of getting out of the lake, and they decided to put the following stratagem into effect. Many of the men embarked in canoes, as if intending to land, and came ashore under the shelter of the trees. But most of them in fact lay flat on their bellies at the bottom of the canoes and so returned to the ships, without more than three or four men being visible on the return journey. Various trips like this were made from all the ships, so that the Spaniards became convinced the rovers intended a night attack on the fort with scaling-ladders. In consequence, they made great preparations for defending the fort from the landward side, bringing all the artillery to bear in that direction.

Night came, and the moon shone bright. The buccaneers were all ready: they slipped anchor and let the ships drift with the tide until they came level with the fort – then they clapped on all sail and sped with the land wind behind them beyond the bar. Instantly the Spaniards shifted part of their artillery round to the seaward side, but the rovers were almost out of reach by then, so little damage was done. Moreover, the Spaniards dared not bring all their big guns to face the sea, fearing that, while they were concentrating their fire in this direction, another band of rovers might be approaching overland to attack them.

Next day Morgan sent a canoe to the fort, bringing back some of the prisoners, whom the Spaniards had given up for dead. He also gave a barque to the rest of the prisoners and let them sail off in it – all except the hostages from Gibraltar, who had not been liberated. Morgan did not choose to let these men go, that they might be an example to the Spaniards for another occasion. He also fired off seven salvoes in farewell to the fort – but his salute was not answered.

The following day the buccaneers were caught in a storm which blew up from the north-east. The fleet dropped anchor in five fathom of water, but the sea was so rough the anchors could not hold, so they were forced to sail on. Some of the vessels had sprung leaks and they were in great peril. They dared not put in to the shore, for they could expect mercy neither from the Spaniards nor the Indians if they fell into their hands. At last the gale began to die out, after they had passed many days in extreme danger.

While Morgan had acquired good booty and won a great victory over the Spaniards, his fellow buccaneers, who had left him near Cabo de Lobos to go and plunder the English ship, had suffered a terrible beating at Comanago on the coast of Caracas. They had come to the rendezvous on the island of Savona, but failed to find the letter Morgan had left for them inside a jar. As they did not know where Morgan had gone to, they decided to attack some place on their own. They were about 500 strong, and had five ships and a barque. They chose for their leader a certain Captain Ansel, who had conducted himself valiantly in the capture of Porto Bello, and decided that the town of Comanago should be their objective. This town lies on the mainland coast of the province of Caracas, about sixty leagues west of Trinidad.

On arrival, the rovers came on shore in their usual manner, and killed some Indians who were on the beach. But when they reached the town, they were surrounded on every side by Spaniards and Indians. They had no thoughts of booty, but only of how to get back to the shore. Nevertheless, the rovers put up a determined fight, and won back to the ships again – but not as whole as they had set out, for they left more than 100 dead, and had fifty wounded men among them.

When they reached Jamaica once more, the buccaneers who had been with Morgan mocked and jeered at them, asking what sort of coins were struck in Comanago.

PART THREE

*The capture and burning of Panama City,
on the South Sea, by Morgan;
with the capture of other places besides;
together with the voyage of the author
along the coast of Costa Rica
and the events of this journey.*

*

CHAPTER ONE

*Morgan comes to Hispaniola to prepare a new fleet
for attacks on the Spanish coast.*

IT is a matter of common observation that success spurs on the
soldier to enhance his glory, the merchant to increase his
riches, and the artist to augment his knowledge. So it was
with Morgan, when he saw all his undertakings crowned
with success: he began to think of still greater exploits, where
luck and prosperity would always attend him. We shall now
give an account of his latest voyages, in which the curious
reader shall see how God permitted the unrighteousness
of the buccaneers to flourish, for the chastisement of the
Spaniards.

When Morgan saw that his men had squandered the Maracaibo booty and were just as badly off as before, he thought of
a new enterprise, knowing he would have little trouble in
persuading them to a fresh attack on the Spanish coast. He
gave them a rendezvous on the south side of Tortuga, and
wrote letters to the governor there, and to all the planters and
hunters of Hispaniola. He told them his intention was to
gather together a force capable of attacking some place of
importance, where they all – once the battle was fought and
won – would make their fortunes.

Once they had received this letter, the buccaneers of Tortuga and Hispaniola eagerly sought to join Morgan's fleet. The
success of his former voyages and the friendship he always
showed towards the French made him popular even with
those who had never set eyes on him. Every buccaneer ship
in Tortuga was instantly made ready, and took on as many
men as it could hold. Those who could not get a place in these
ships took to their canoes and sailed along the coast to join
Morgan's fleet and embark on the English ships. Others made

their way overland through the forest to the south coast of the island to join the expedition.

On 24 October 1670, Morgan arrived at a harbour the French call Port Couillon, on the south of Hispaniola opposite Isla de la Vaca, which was the place of rendezvous. Finding most of his force assembled, he held a council to discuss the best means of obtaining provisions. Morgan suggested sending out four ships and a barque, with 400 men, to loot maize from the villages along the mainland coast. The captains agreed, and so did the men when the proposal was put to them. It was decided to go to Rio de la Hacha and assault a little town called la Rancheria, where most maize is to be found and where they might possibly encounter the barques which come there from Cartagena to fish pearls.

Buccaneers from the ships not going on this expedition were sent into the woods to hunt animals and salt the meat, while others careened the ships and did any repairs which were necessary.

CHAPTER TWO

The expedition to Rio de la Hacha.

Six days after the four buccaneer ships had sailed from Hispaniola, when they were in sight of Rio de la Hacha, they were becalmed. The Spaniards could see them off shore, and immediately began to arm. They were not sure that the ships intended to land but, being accustomed to the rovers' frequent depredations, they took the precaution of hiding their goods – always their first consideration – so that if they got the worst of any encounter they could escape in good time.

There was a ship in port from Cartagena, come to load maize, which intended to slip out with the land wind that night and escape the rovers, but it had no such luck: the buccaneer fleet closed in around it. This capture suited them excellently, for the ship was laden with the very thing they were looking for – maize.

At break of day the fleet came as close inshore as possible, in order to land the men. The landing was effected despite stiff resistance from the Spaniards, who had thrown up breastworks on the beach. They were forced to abandon these defences and retire to the village, yet still with hopes of driving off the raiders. When the buccaneers reached the village the battle began anew and lasted till evening, when the Spaniards gave it up and fled. They had lost many men, and inflicted little damage on the invaders.

When the buccaneers entered the village they saw the Spaniards had left them nothing but empty houses, having carried off all the goods. The rovers immediately set off in pursuit. They overtook one party of fugitives and took them prisoner. Next day the captives were tortured, as usual, to make them reveal where their money and goods were hidden; some confessed and others kept silence.

The buccaneers began sending out marauding parties and managed to collect plenty of booty and numerous slaves. The Spaniards, who dared not forsake the shelter of the forest, set up various ambushes in an attempt to shake off the invaders – but to no avail. The more harm they did to the rovers, the more it redounded on their own heads when they were captured.

When the buccaneers had been a fortnight at this village and had plundered all they could possibly lay hands on, they decided to return to their companions in Hispaniola. They therefore let the Spaniards of Rio de la Hacha know that a ransom must be produced for their village. The Spaniards said that they would rather let the village be burnt, and that they had no money to give. The rovers, who would as soon have had maize as money on this occasion, said they would settle for a quantity of maize in payment. The Spaniards were not over-willing to do this, either, but when they saw the rovers intended to burn down the village, they complied. They agreed to produce 4,000 *fanegas* of maize (about 200 tons), which they collected with all speed, the sooner to be rid of the buccaneers. Within three days the buccaneers were at sea, with all their booty and the captured slaves on board, steering for Hispaniola where the main body of the fleet awaited them.

Five weeks had gone by since the expedition had set sail, and Morgan had begun to have doubts whether they would ever return. He did not know what to think – they might have taken some rich prize and absconded with it, or perhaps they had suffered a defeat, for the place they had set out to attack was within reach of help from Cartagena or Santa Maria, and there were always some ships out of Cartagena cruising against the rovers. Morgan was just on the point of making other plans when he saw the ships approaching, with a greater number than had set out. Morgan was immensely delighted, and so were all his companions, and their joy was further enhanced when they were told the ships were all laden with maize.

Morgan's ships were ready to sail, and had only been waiting for the return of these vessels. They were unloaded at once, and the hunters were recalled from the woods to come on board. While the newly arrived ships were also being made ready for sea, the salt meat was got on board as quickly as could be, and the maize was shared out among all the ships, according to the number of men. Morgan gave Cabo Tiburon, on the western point of Hispaniola, as the rendezvous, where they would resolve which place to attack.

They all reached this destination shortly afterwards, and were also joined by some more ships from Jamaica, which had been seeking Morgan's fleet. This now consisted of thirty-seven ships and several other smaller vessels; the entire complement of men was about 2,000 all well armed with muskets, pistols and cutlasses, together with powder, bullets and other munitions. The ships too were well equipped with guns, according to their size. The admiral's ship was the heaviest, and mounted twenty-two cannon and six brass swivels. The number of guns on the other ships ranged from twenty, eighteen, sixteen, fourteen down to four on the smallest vessels. They were also well provided with gunpowder, hand grenades and other explosive missiles.

After Morgan, as admiral, had made a thorough inspection and seen there was nothing lacking, he divided the fleet into two squadrons, under two different flags – the English flag and the white flag – and appointed officers, such as vice-admirals and rear-admirals, to command them. He issued commissions to all the ships not already provided with them, permitting all acts of violence against the Spanish dominions and the capture of Spanish ships, at sea or in harbour, according to the right of reprisals, as overt enemies of the English crown, since the Spaniards seized all English ships which entered their harbours merely to take on water or other necessities.

Having put everything in good order, Morgan invited all the captains and leading officers of his fleet to a conference to agree on the sum of money he should receive for his generalship. All the officers assembled, and voted that Morgan should receive a share of one-hundredth of the proceeds. This proposal was then made known to the crews, who also gave it their vote. Then a general agreement was drawn up as to what the captains should receive for their ships. The other officers – the lieutenants and bos'ns – assembled and voted that the captains should be given the value of eight men's portions for for their ship, as well as their own personal share. The surgeons would receive 200 pieces of eight for furnishing their medicine chests, in addition to their personal share like every man on board. The carpenters would get an extra 100 pieces of eight.

Then the rewards were stated for those who behaved with extraordinary gallantry – such as being the first to tear down the flag on a fort and run up the English colours. This would earn an extra fifty pieces of eight, while a man who brought in a prisoner when intelligence was needed would have an extra 200. As for the grenadiers, they were to receive five pieces of eight extra for every grenade they threw into a fort.

Compensations were also laid down for those mutilated in battle. A man who lost both legs would receive 1,500 pieces of eight over and above his ordinary share, or he could choose fifteen slaves instead. A man who lost both hands was to have 1,800 pieces of eight, or eighteen slaves, whichever he preferred.

For the loss of one leg, either right or left, a man was to be awarded 600 pieces of eight or six slaves. For the loss of either hand, the same compensation was offered. If a man lost an eye or a finger, he would receive 100 pieces of eight, or one slave. As recompense for the pain of a body wound which necessitated the insertion of a pipe, the amount was 500 pieces of eight, or five slaves. For a stiff limb, be it arm, leg or finger, a man received the same compensation as if he had lost it entirely.

All these rewards and compensations were to be taken out of the common booty, before this was divided up. These articles were agreed by unanimous vote and then signed – first by Morgan, then by all the captains and officers of the fleet.

Having taken care of all this business, Morgan held a council of war with the ships' captains to decide where first to attack. It was proposed that they attack one of these three places: Cartagena, Panama or Vera Cruz. There was no argument about whether the buccaneer force was sufficient, or which place was most strongly defended – none of the three was judged to be as rich as Panama and therefore by common consent it was decided that this should be the main goal to attack and plunder. To this end, St Catalina should first be invaded, in order to secure a guide who could show us [*sic*] the way to Panama, as felons from all parts of the coast are sent to that island.

A special article was also drawn up: ships taken at sea or in port would form part of the general share-out, but there would be a prize of 1,000 pieces of eight for the buccaneers who first boarded an enemy vessel. If the captured ship proved to be worth more than 10,000 pieces of eight, the reward would be one-tenth of the value.

Boarding any ship other than an enemy was forbidden on pain of death, so that news of their raid should not spread.

CHAPTER THREE

Morgan and his fleet leave Hispaniola and capture
St Catalina.

THE buccaneer fleet under Morgan's command, well provided with all things needful for the voyage, put to sea on 16 December 1670. Four days later they sighted St Catalina, an island – as I have previously mentioned – occupied by a Spanish garrison, and the place of banishment for all the felons of the region. It is a mountainous island about seven leagues in circumference, three leagues long and one broad, situated at latitude 13° 20′ north, about 100 leagues from Cartagena and sixty-two from Porto Bello, in the same longitude as Rio de Chagre. There is no game on the island except at a certain season when wild pigeons come in great multitudes. There are four rivers, two of which dry up in summer. No trading is done; the inhabitants plant only what they need to live on, although the land would be suitable enough for planting tobacco.

On approaching the island, Morgan sent ahead a fast sailing ship mounting fourteen guns to keep watch on the entrance to the port and prevent any vessel that might be in harbour from slipping out to the mainland to give warning of the buccaneers.

Early next morning the whole fleet came to anchor below the island, near a place called Aguada Grande, where the Spaniards had formerly mounted a battery of four cannon. Morgan landed with a force of about 1,000 men, and, when all were ranged in proper order, they began to march through the woods. As yet they had no guides except those of their own company who had been on this island when Mansveldt invaded it. In the evening they came to a place which had been the governor's residence in the old days, where there was a battery known as Plataforma St Jago, but there was nobody there. The Spaniards, to conserve their defences more easily, had retired to the small island adjoining, which is so close a bridge could span the two. They had girdled this island with forts and batteries, so that it seemed impregnable.

When the buccaneers came in sight, they were met with heavy fire from the cannon on the small island, although few shots found their mark. Darkness fell at last, and the buccaneers could advance no farther. They slept out under the stars, according to their old habit, with no surfeit of supper in their stomachs – for they'd eaten nothing all day. At about one o'clock at night, heavy rain began to fall and continued a long time. The rovers pulled down a few huts and made a bonfire to warm themselves, for the rain was bitterly cold and they could hardly endure it. They were not thickly clad, having on nothing more than a shirt and a pair of breeches, without stockings or shoes, which did not give them much warmth.

The rain began to ease off at daybreak and the rovers began cleaning their weapons – which were in a bad state, for most had got wet. In fact, if 100 well armed men had come upon them that night, they could easily have overcome the whole buccaneer force. Having dried and primed their muskets they began the march once more, but the rain came on again worse than before, and at this point the Spaniards renewed their bombardment, to demonstrate that their powder was not wet.

The rovers dared not attack the fortresses in the rain, and looked about for any houses where they could protect their weapons from the heavy deluge. Everybody was busy making huts of grass or branches. Amidst all this discomfort they began to feel so desperately hungry they had to find food of some sort. There was an old horse which the Spaniards had turned loose because it was no longer fit for work, as its back was full of open sores. This beast they shot dead, and everyone who could grabbed himself a bit, roasted it a little over the fire and ate it up as though it had been the most delectable dish you could possibly wish for – yes, and a man had to be quick off the mark to get hold of such a morsel.

Still the rain kept on, and Morgan saw that his men were grumbling and wanting to go back to the ships. He sent a canoe over to the Spaniards, under a white flag, summoning them to give up the island, threatening that he would give no quarter if they would not surrender willingly.

Close on midday, the canoe returned with the governor's answer, in which he requested two hours' grace while he deliberated with his officers. After this time, there came a canoe from the Spaniards, flying the flag of truce and carrying two persons to arrange the capitulation. Before they landed, they requested two hostages in exchange for the two who were to parley with Morgan. He sent out two captains in exchange for the major and the ensign who were the Spanish envoys. When the latter had come to Morgan, they said the Spaniards were willing to surrender the island, as their forces were no match for his. However, they begged him, to save their reputations, to be good enough to employ the following ruse.

The buccaneers should cross the bridge joining the two islands at night and storm the fort of St Jeronimo. The ships should be sent round by the fortress of St Teresa, as if to attack the same. Meanwhile, other men were to land from canoes at the St Mateo battery. The governor should be intercepted and taken prisoner on his way from the St Jeronimo fort to the fortress of St Teresa and obliged to surrender this stronghold. When the English attemped to enter, there would be heavy firing on both sides – but in the air, or with blanks, so that no one should suffer from it. Once these two fortifications were in their hands, the rovers would have nothing to fear from the others. The Spaniards furthermore requested that they should be set ashore later at some place on the mainland coast, wherever Morgan pleased, so long as they could only join their own people.

Morgan agreed to all their proposals, on condition that none of his men should lose his life or suffer any injury – or else the buccaneers would give no quarter. The Spaniards assured him that no harm should come of it, and returned to their governor.

Morgan at once gave orders for his ships to come into port, as the governor had enjoined, and told his men to prepare to storm the fort of St Jeronimo. By evening, all the forts on the little island were in process of being conquered, in the manner the Spaniards had proposed to Morgan. However, despite the agreement to fire blanks, Morgan had ordered his men to use live ammunition, but on no account to fire on the Spaniards unless the defenders shot at them.

The mock battle went on: there was vigorous firing on both sides from the heavy artillery, and skirmishing with small-arms, without injury to anyone. Finally, the buccaneers entered the small island in the dark of night, took possession of all the defences and made all the Spaniards go into the church. The governor was ordered to keep all his people together: any Spaniards found on the streets would be shot.

When all was calm, and the compact with the Spaniards had been carried out, the war against the hens and pigs and sheep began – boiling and roasting went on all night. When short of wood, they pulled down houses for fuel. Getting food was everybody's main concern. Some, when they were satisfied, took what remained of their meal to the church, where they gave some to the Spanish women, but the men had to look on.

Early next morning the people on the island were counted. There were about 450 altogether, including 190 men from the garrison; forty married couples, with forty-three children; thirty-one slaves of his majesty, with eight children; eight convicts; thirty-nine Negroes belonging to private owners, with twenty-two children; twenty-seven other Negroes with twelve children. The Spaniards were all disarmed; the men were allowed to go to the plantations to get food, but the women were kept shut up in the church.

Then all the island's fortifications were inspected. The fort of St Jeronimo, which commanded the bridge, had eight cannon, firing balls of twelve, eight and six pounds; six pipes of muskets (ten in each) and sixty other muskets, together with gunpowder, bullets and fuses. The second battery, called Plataforma de St Mateo, had three eight-pounders. The third and most important defence was the fortress of St Teresa. This was equipped with twenty cannon, firing balls of twelve, eight and six pounds; ten pipes of muskets (each containing ten) and ninety muskets besides, together with grenades, gunpowder, shot and fuses. This fortress was built of stone and mortar, the walls very thick, and surrounded by a dry moat a good twenty feet deep, accessible only by a drawbridge. In the middle of the fortress was a walled mound, mounting four cannon, which commanded the harbour and the island around. The sea pounded terrifyingly against the cliffs on the seaward side, making the fortress unassailable. On the landward side it could be approached only by a path no more than three or four paces wide, with steep rocky valleys plunging down on either side.

The fourth battery, Plataforma de St Augustin, had three cannon, firing balls of eight and six pounds; the fifth, de la Concepcion, had two eight-pounders. The Plataforma de Nuestra Señora de Guadalupe had two twelve-pounders; San Salvador had two eight-pounders; de los Artilleros, two six-pounders. Three cannon firing balls of eight and six pounds were mounted at Plataforma Santa Cruz. The final defence was the fort of St Jose, where there were six cannon, firing balls of twelve and eight pounds; two pipes of ten musket barrels each, twenty other muskets, together with the necessary powder, bullets and fuses.

The buccaneers also found a magazine containing over 30,000 pounds of gunpowder and other munitions. All these military supplies were carried aboard the ships. The batteries and the fort of St Jose were all abandoned; the guns were spiked and the gun-carriages burnt. Only the fortress of St Teresa and the St Jeronimo fort were maintained and guarded.

When Morgan had put everything in order, he had the prisoners questioned to find if there were any convicts from Panama or Porto Bello among them. Three came forward who were very familiar with those parts. Morgan persuasively asked them whether they were willing to be his guides and show his forces the way to Panama, promising to set them free and take them back with him to Jamaica, with as much booty as they could gather. This suited the convicts very well, and they promised to serve him faithfully. One of them, a half-breed, showed particular eagerness, as he hoped to use this opportunity to revenge the wrong he thought had been done him – as indeed it had, for he did not deserve banishment, but rather to have been broken alive on the wheel for all the murders, rapes and robberies he had committed. This scoundrel coerced the other two, who were Indians, born in the Spanish dominions and very well acquainted with the roads, threatening to have them burnt alive if they would not serve the buccaneers. He told Morgan these men were essential as guides: if necessary, they must be beaten into obedience.

Having found what he'd been seeking, Morgan and his chief officers decided to equip four ships and a barque to attack the fortress at the mouth of the river Chagre. They did not wish to arouse the suspicion of the Spaniards by the appearance of the entire fleet, lest warning should be sent to Panama. Four hundred men were selected to go on the expedition to capture Fort Chagre.

We too will leave Morgan and the rest of his men on St Catalina, and accompany these four ships to see how they made themselves masters of the fortress.

CHAPTER FOUR

The capture of the fortress San Lorenzo de Chagre.

THE commander of the expedition was Brodely, a man with a long career of marauding in these regions. Three days after leaving St Catalina the four ships sighted the fortress of Chagre, standing on a high mountain at the mouth of the river. The summit is intersected by a moat, a good thirty feet deep, which can be crossed at one place only, where there is a drawbridge. The fortress is surrounded by strong palisades, filled in with earth. Four bastions command the landward side, and two face the sea. To the south, the mountain is so steep it is impossible to climb, and to the north lies the river. A tower, mounted with eight cannon, defends the entry of the river, and somewhat lower down are two more batteries, each with six cannon, defending the river banks.

Nearby are various warehouses, where the munitions and supplies are stored. Beside these warehouses is a stairway, hewn out of the mountain-side, by which one ascends to the fortress. To the west of the fort is a harbour for small vessels, where the water is three, four and seven fathoms deep. In front of the fortress is a good anchorage, of seven and eight fathoms, and at the mouth of the river lies a reef over which the water breaks.

When the Spaniards saw the buccaneer ships, they began firing on them with heavy artillery from the fortress. The rovers dropped anchor in a little harbour, about a league away, and came ashore next morning at daybreak, intending to approach through the woods, capture the fortress, and then bring their ships into the river. They were on the march from dawn till two in the afternoon before they could come near the fort, as the forest tracks were impassable, full of quagmires or blocked by enormous boulders. They had to hack their way through, for the thickly entwined creepers made advance impossible. Some slaves they had brought with them from St Catalina were very useful in cleaving a passage.

When they did reach the fortress, they were instantly greeted by intense artillery fire from the Spaniards within. The rovers suffered heavy damage as they were completely exposed, for in order to storm the fortress they had to break cover. The defenders could see them from head to foot, whereas the rovers were unable to get a glimpse of the Spaniards. They were in great anxiety, not knowing how best to set about the attack. This was going to be a hard nut to crack, yet they dared not turn back and be disgraced in the eyes of their fellows. They resolved to assault the fortress, come what may.

They made a vigorous assault with muskets and hand grenades, but the Spaniards had such good cover the rovers could do them little damage. They returned the fire furiously with cannon and muskets, shouting at the attackers: '*Vengan los demas, perros ingleses, enemigos de dios y del rey; vos no habeis de ir a Panama.*' That is to say: 'Let the others come too, you English dogs, enemies of God and the King – you shall not get to Panama.' Finally, the buccaneers were forced to retire.

In the evening they advanced again, intending to throw in hand-grenades and then scale the palisades, but failed in the attempt. One of the buccaneers was pierced through the shoulder by an arrow; in a fury he wrenched it out, took a wad of cotton from his pouch, tied it to the arrowhead and set fire to it. When it was well alight, he stuck the arrow in his musket and shot it into the palm-leaf thatch of some houses within the fortress walls. The other buccaneers, seeing his idea, began to do the same. At last, they succeeded in setting the roofs of two or three houses on fire.

The defenders apparently were so busy they did not notice this until the burning thatch came crashing down on them, igniting a cask of gunpowder and putting most of the Spaniards out of action. The buccaneers made the most of their opportunity and renewed the assault. The Spaniards were doing all they could to extinguish the fire, but could not get sufficient water to check the spreading blaze, for the buildings were nearly all of dry wood. A fresh breeze was blowing, which did not help matters.

Meanwhile the buccaneers, seeing the fire increase within the fortress walls, endeavoured to set the outer palisades ablaze. The attempt succeeded, although not without great trouble and the loss of many men, for when the Spaniards realized their enemies were in the moat, they hurled down pots of gunpowder with lighted fuses attached. These missiles worked great havoc among the attackers, but they achieved their objective notwithstanding. By nightfall the palisades were burning. The rovers crept on hands and knees close to the blaze, shooting down every Spaniard they glimpsed through the flames.

By daybreak the fire had burnt through the palisades almost completely. The earth rampart which they had supported started to collapse, and as the ground gave way under the guns they too pitched down into the moat. The buccaneers could concentrate their fire on the Spaniards now exposed to view. The governor of the fortress kept his men under such discipline that they dare not withdraw; he had artillery brought into the breach made by the fire so that resistance could continue. Yet the defenders' spirits sank, now they no longer had proper cover. The rovers kept up such a furious, accurate fire that any Spaniard who dared show himself was instantly shot down.

All this time the fire had been spreading. Once the breach was wide enough, the rovers too tried to quell the flames, fetching earth for the purpose. While one group was busy at this work, the rest attended to the Spaniards. Finally, most of the defenders succumbed, either from the fire or from the rovers' deadly bullets. About midday the buccaneers sprang through the breach, despite the fire, which was still raging, and despite the continued resistance of the governor and some twenty-five of his men. Those whose guns were now useless hurled stones or fought with spears, yet the buccaneers pressed on notwithstanding and at last made themselves masters of the fortress.

The surviving Spaniards leapt down from the wall, without crying for quarter, many of them breaking their necks. The governor retired to a guardhouse where there were two cannon, meaning to resist to the end. He too refused to ask for quarter, and the invaders had no choice but to shoot him dead.

They found about thirty men in the fortress, not ten unwounded among them. These were all that remained of the 314 men who had been in the castle, and not a single officer survived. They told the rovers that eight or nine men had fled to Panama. The prisoners also said that the president of Panama had received information, some three weeks ago, that the English were getting a fleet together on Hispaniola, with the object of taking Panama. The news had been brought, they said, by an Irishman who had run away from the buccaneers at Rio de la Hacha, where they had attacked in order to get provisions for their fleet. In consequence, the president of Panama had sent 164 men to the relief of Fort Chagre, with food supplies and munitions of war. The original garrison had been 150 men, so that, all told, the place had been defended by 314 well-armed men.

The prisoners also informed the buccaneers that the president had placed numerous ambuscades along the river, and that he was waiting for us [*sic*] on the savanas of Panama with a force of 2,400 white men, 600 half-breeds and 600 Indians, with 2,000 wild bulls.

The rovers, then, had won the fortress – but it had not been accomplished so easily as the conquest of St Catalina. They counted their dead, and found they had lost more than a hundred, and that sixty of their men were wounded. They made the prisoners throw down the Spanish corpses from the mountain to the shore, and dig graves for the dead buccaneers. The wounded were carried inside the church, where the women prisoners were kept. When all this had been done, they set about repairing the damage done by the fire.

Morgan, who had stayed on St Catalina, did not remain there long after the departure of the four ships. He had all the food supplies – such as maize and cassava – put on board his vessels for the maintenance of the garrison he intended to leave in Fort Chagre. His plan was to arrive there a day or two after the capture of the fortress and then immediately to march on Panama, thus giving the Spaniards no time to prepare much resistance.

As rapidly as possible, therefore, he had all the ordnance of the forts on St Catalina cast into the water, yet in a place where he knew he could recover it at need – for he still had the notion of returning some day or other, to hold the island as a base for the buccaneers. All the buildings were set on fire, except the fortress, to which little damage was done.

All the prisoners were put on board, and then Morgan and his fleet set their course for Rio de Chagre. Here they arrived eight days after the capture of the fortress. When he saw the English flag waving from the wall, Morgan was in such a hurry to enter the river that he ran his ship aground on a reef which lies at the river mouth. Three others of his companion ships also came to grief there, but without loss of life; they still had time enough, after the ships had struck, to salvage their goods. In fact they might well have rescued the ships themselves, had it not been for a strong north wind rising, which dashed the ships to pieces, washing them up high and dry on the shore.

Having entered the fortress and been informed of what had gone on, Morgan immediately set all the prisoners to work repairing the fort, and had new palisades erected around the outworks. There were several of those vessels in the river which the Spaniards call *chatas* – flat-bottomed boats used for carrying goods upriver. They are poled along, like the Dutch barges, and sometimes go as far as Porto Bello and Nicaragua. Morgan had each mounted with two guns and four swivels. Besides these, four rowing boats and all the ships' canoes were made ready for the journey upriver. Five hundred men were ordered to stay in the fortress, and 150 were left on the buccaneer ships which lay in the river. The rest, 1,200 strong, received orders to advance on Panama. They took no food supplies with them in the boats, hoping to find victuals in plenty at the places where the enemy had set up ambuscades.

CHAPTER FIVE

Morgan leaves Fort Chagre, and advances on
Panama with twelve hundred men.

MORGAN, having paid close attention to all these matters –
taken good care of the fortress and supplied his men with
every sort of military equipment available – left the river
Chagre and commenced his journey to Panama on 18 January
1670. He had five vessels mounting guns, as well as thirty-
two canoes, all fully manned. This is an account of what
happened day by day, from the time he left Chagre to his
arrival in Panama City.

That day, they sailed or rowed upriver for about six leagues,
and in the evening reached a place called Rio de Dos Brazos.
A party of men went ashore to bivouac, for the ships were so
crowded they could not sleep aboard in comfort. The buccaneers had hoped to find something to eat in the plantations,
but the Spaniards had taken everything, and left the houses
completely empty. So they went to sleep in hopes of making
good tomorrow the damage their stomachs had suffered that
day. In the meantime, those who had such a thing had to be
content with a pipe of tobacco.

On the second day, they all set forth at daybreak, and about
noon reached a place called La Cruz de San Juan Gallego.
Here the buccaneers were forced to leave the five ships,
because the river had dried up as no rain had fallen for a long
time, and several trees had fallen across the river bed, blocking
the passage of large vessels.

Two or three leagues farther on, so the guides told us, one
party of men could march overland, and the rest continue in
the canoes. In case the enemy should show in force and turn
us back, some men were ordered that evening to stay aboard
the ships, so that these could be used as a refuge, and if neces-

sary cover the retreat with their cannon. A hundred and sixty men stayed behind, under strict orders not to land. This was lest the enemy take prisoners, and thereby discover the strength of the buccaneer force.

Next day – the third day – a squad of men and a guide were sent ahead to try to find an overland route, and warned to look out for ambushes, as the forest was dense and almost impenetrable. They found nothing but swamp, and were unable to get through. Morgan was obliged to send one part of his command in the canoes to a place called Cedro Bueno. That evening the canoes came back, and carried the rest of the men on. The buccaneers were by now deathly faint with hunger. They desperately longed for an encounter with the enemy, so that they might then get hold of some food.

On the fourth day, the larger part of the buccaneer expedition marched inland across the Isthmus, with one of the guides. The remainder, with another guide, went upriver in canoes – two canoes proceeding about three musket-shots ahead of the others, to guard against Spanish ambuscades. The Spaniards also had their scouts, observing every move the rovers made. They were able to outstrip the invaders and warn the defenders in good time, before the buccaneers could take them by surprise.

About noon the rovers reached a place called Torno Caballos, where the men in the two advance canoes had warned them they would encounter a Spanish ambuscade. The buccaneers had at once got ready for the fight with as much zeal and joy as if they'd been invited to a marriage feast. Food and drink were extremely scarce among them, and at Torno Caballos they hoped to find both in abundance. They were ready to trample each other under foot, each wanting to be first. But the birds had flown, leaving the nest empty apart from about 150 leather bags which had once contained meat and bread. A few crumbs remained, of no use among so many.

They tore apart the huts put up by the Spaniards, but, since they found nothing better, the buccaneers ate the leather bags, with as much gusto as if leather were meat – and so it was, in their imagination. They even fought over it. The man who started with a whole bag was lucky to be left with a scrap for himself.

About 500 men were estimated to have been withdrawn from that ambush. After the buccaneers had rested there a while, and stayed their hunger with the leather, they marched on once more and by evening came to a place called Torno Muni. Here was the site of yet another ambuscade, also deserted. This had raised false hopes among them, rather than alarm, because they had been eagerly looking forward to an encounter with the Spaniards, in expectation of coming across something to eat.

Having passed by these two ambuscades, they dispersed into the forest, looking for food – but to no avail. The Spaniards had left nothing behind. Those who had saved a bit of leather from the first place of ambush had it for supper, washed down with water. Some curious readers, whose lives have never taken them far from their mother's kitchen, thinking leather inedible may wish to know how the rovers managed. They beat the leather between two stones at the water's edge, made it wet, and scraped off the hair while it was soft. Then, having roasted it on hot embers, they cut it up in small pieces which they swallowed whole.

On the fifth day, the buccaneers were again on the march at dawn. About noon they reached Barba Coa, a place where another ambush had been abandoned. They searched the near-by plantations for something to appease their hunger, but once again the Spaniards had stripped all bare.

At last, after ferreting everywhere, they came across a newly-dug pit, and in it found two sacks of meal, two big bottles of wine and some plantains. Morgan could see that some of his men, stricken with hunger, had become extremely weak, so he had these provisions shared among those who most needed them. After eating, they were able once more to march, but those too weak to make much headway were put in the canoes, while those who so far had travelled by canoe went on by land. All day they tramped onward, until darkness fell, when they came to a plantation where they bivouacked for the night. Here, as elsewhere, the Spaniards had carried off all the food.

The sixth day – after a night sleepless with hunger – they set off as before, one party marching, the other in the canoes. Often they were obliged to stop and rest – and everyone then scoured the woods for something to eat. Some tried chewing leaves and berries from the trees, others in their desperation ate grass seeds. About noon they came upon a plantation where there was a barn full of maize. At once the barn was demolished, and each man took all the maize his hands could hold, and devoured it on the spot.

When the rest of the maize had been shared out among them, they continued their march, but a league farther on ran into an Indian ambush. Expecting to find food there as well as men, they let their maize drop and rushed headlong for the place where the Indians had been seen.

They found there neither Indians nor victuals, but saw about 100 Indians on the far side of the river, running away. Some of the buccaneers dived in and swam across, resolved if they shot an Indian and found he carried no rations, to eat him up instead. But the Indians, already deep in the wood, were laughing at them. They managed to shoot two or three of their pursuers, killing one, and called out, '*Ha, perros – a la savana, a la savana.*' ('To the open field, you dogs – wait till we meet you on the open field.')

By that evening, the buccaneers could go no farther, since to continue their march they would be obliged to cross the river. They began to grouse among themselves. Some, who wanted to turn back, were shouted down by the braver ones. But all took heart when they heard one of the guides say they were near a village which would put up a fight, and where there would certainly be stores of food.

Next morning, on the seventh day, the buccaneers cleaned their weapons, firing off their muskets to make sure they would be in good order when they went into action. Then,

leaving Santa Cruz, where they had encamped, they crossed
the river by canoe. When all were lined up on the far bank
they again marched off, itching for a fight in the hope, as I
have said, that it might mean food.

About midday they came near the village, which was called
Cruz, and could see great plumes of smoke rising. At once they
began to cheer up, joking to each other that the Spaniards
had put the spit on the fire in readiness for their arrival. But
when they reached the village, though fires were burning true
enough, there was neither meat nor drink for them. The
Spaniards had set all the buildings alight, except the royal
storehouse and stables. All their animals had been driven off,
and no living creature was encountered but a few stray dogs,
which the buccaneers shot and ate.

In the royal storehouse they found fifteen or sixteen jars of
Peruvian wine, and a sack of bread. The moment they discovered the wine the buccaneers began drinking, but on top
of all the rubbish they had eaten on the march – leaves of
trees and other indigestible stuff – it made them extremely
sick. Not understanding why, they thought the Spaniards
must have poisoned the wine.

That day they could go no farther, and had to pass the night
in the burnt out ruins of Cruz. The village lies 9° 20′ north,
sixteen leagues from the river Chagre and eight from Panama.
There are storehouses in Cruz because it is the highest navig-
able point upriver, and merchandise is stored there to be
carried on to Panama by pack mule.

Morgan too had to leave his canoes there. Henceforth, all
the men would have to march. He decided he would send the
canoes back to the place where the ships were moored, except
for one kept hidden near by, to take a message in an
emergency.

Several Indians and Spaniards had been seen in the plantations near Cruz, so Morgan ordered that no one should leave
the village, except by companies 100 strong. Nevertheless
many of the buccaneers, driven by hunger, disobeyed, going
off in groups of no more than half a dozen to search the

plantations for food. The Indians and Spaniards, on the alert, fell on one of these foraging parties and managed to take a prisoner. The others got away and told Morgan, but he kept the news secret so as not to depress the spirits of his men. Vigilant watch was kept at night in case of attack.

On the eighth day, Morgan and his men advanced along the road to Panama City, the 200 best equipped buccaneers marching in the vanguard, on the look-out for ambuscades. The narrow road crossed difficult country, ideal for this form of warfare. Not more than twelve men could march abreast, sometimes fewer. After ten hours on the march, the buccaneers had reached a place called Quebrada Oscura, when in a sudden surprise attack, three or four thousand arrows were loosed off at them. The vanguard had seen no enemy. They were marching up a mountainside, where a track had been hacked out wide enough for a pack mule to pass. The buccaneers panicked, for their foe was invisible and the arrows fell as thick as hail. They fired wildly into the woods, then some of them began aiming at the Indians who could now be glimpsed moving through the trees uphill to lie in wait for the column farther on and mount a second attack.

One band of Indians stood their ground and fought, until at last their chief fell wounded. Yet even then he tried to rise and run a buccaneer through the body with his spear – but was shot before he could land the blow, and fell amid three or four other Indian dead. Though the buccaneers tried to take prisoners they had no luck, because the Indians were quicker on their feet. In this encounter, eight rovers were killed and ten wounded – but not one of them would have come through had the Indians shown more courage. They shot their arrows under cover of the woods, where the boughs of trees often deflected them or made them miss their mark.

The buccaneers came shortly afterwards to a wide stretch of grassland, where they had a good view all around. They saw several Indians on a hilltop near the road they must pass. While the wounded were being seen to, fifty of the best runners were sent ahead after these Indians, to see if they could take a prisoner, but in vain. When the buccaneers had gone some way farther, the Indians once more came in sight, shouting, '*A la savana, a la savana, cornudos, perros ingleses.*' ('To the open field, you cuckolds, you English dogs.')

They were on one hill and the buccaneers on another, with a wooded valley between, where presumably the Indians had set another ambush. Morgan therefore sent 200 men on ahead, and waited on the hillside with the others. As the buccaneers approached, the enemy (either Indians or Spaniards) also went down towards the valley, as if to join battle – but once hidden from sight they slipped away through the forest, letting the buccaneers go onward unmolested.

That evening it began to rain, so to keep their weapons and powder dry the buccaneers left the track and sought for shelter. Hoping to starve them out, the Indians had burnt all the dwellings along the way, and driven off the cattle. Even so, a few undamaged huts were found, and though there was nothing in them to eat, the buccaneers were in better spirits than before.

There was no room in the huts for everyone, but a few from each company were detailed to go under cover, taking their comrades' weapons, which they piled so that in case of need each man could lay hands on his own. The others lay down outside, but got little sleep, for it did nothing but rain all night long.

Next day, the ninth, Morgan set out at dawn in the cool, for going would be difficult since there was no cover from the intense heat of the sun. An hour or two later, about twenty Spaniards were seen ahead of the buccaneers, keeping them under observation. Once again, an attempt to take prisoners failed, for the enemy made such cunning use of the country that often they were behind when the buccaneers supposed them to be in front, and all the time they kept their distance.

At last the buccaneers came to a mountain, and there, ahead, was the South Sea, and a galleon and five or six coasting craft, sailing from Panama City to the islands of Tobago and Tobagilla. All began to take heart. They felt even better when they debouched down the mountainside to a great plain, covered with cattle.

At once they broke ranks and shot down every beast within range. All got busy: while some hunted, others lit fires to roast the meat. One gang of men dragged in a bull, another a cow, a third a horse or a mule. The animals were hacked up and thrown, dripping with blood, on to the fire to cook. The meat scarcely had time to get hot before they grabbed it and began gnawing, gore running down their cheeks.

In the very midst of this good meal, Morgan sounded the stand-to. Each man leapt up at once and ran to his post, not letting go his lump of roast meat, however. Soon they were in marching order, and a party of fifty men was sent ahead to endeavour to take prisoners, as Morgan was by now very concerned at lacking intelligence as to the strength of the Spaniards. Towards evening, this advance guard caught sight of about two hundred of the enemy, who shouted to them, but they could not understand the words, and then passed beyond them out of view.

A little farther on, the buccaneers came in actual sight of the roofs and spires of Panama City. They gave three cheers and threw their caps into the air for joy, as if they had already gained the victory. It was decided to sleep there, and march down on Panama in the morning. They pitched camp on the plain, and began to beat the drums and blow the trumpets and wave their flags, as if at a celebration.

As the drums and trumpets sounded, fifty horsemen rode up with a trumpeter of their own, and halted just out of range. The trumpeter blew loud and clear, and the horsemen called out, '*Mañana, mañana, perros, nos veremos.*' ('Tomorrow, you dogs, tomorrow we shall see what happens.') Then all but seven or eight rode off. These kept watch on the buccaneers, who were unconcerned, and went about collecting hay to make palliasses for the night.

The 200 enemy encountered earlier in the day also showed up, and took up positions to block the buccaneers' line of retreat. No one was worried. Those who had meat left over from the feast at midday ate it up, and lay down to rest. Each man knew what to do if the Spaniards attacked. Around the army, if you could call it an army, sentries had been posted. All through the night the Spaniards fired off their big guns from the city.

At dawn on the morning of the tenth day the buccaneers got ready for the assault. Morgan had them drawn up in battle order, and on they marched with drums beating and flags flying. The guides had warned Morgan to take another way, avoiding the high-road, where the Spaniards were sure to have laid an effective ambush. So, a musket-shot to their right, the buccaneers left the main road and filed down a path through the woods. The going was rough, but they were men so used to hardship that it made little difference. Just as the guides had said, the Spaniards were entrenched along the high road, and when they saw the buccaneers going another way they were obliged to turn and meet them.

The Spanish general drew up his army in battle order and marched towards the buccaneers. The Spanish force comprised two squadrons of cavalry and four battalions of foot, together with two herds of wild bulls, goaded along by a mob of Indians, Negroes and half-breeds. The buccaneers were drawn up on a rise, and had a good view of the Spaniards. The rovers were so outnumbered that each man knew he would be lucky to get off with a whole skin, but retreat was impossible. They resolved to fall on the enemy and to fight to the last men, since they knew there would be no quarter for them from the Spaniards.

Once the word had been given, the buccaneers extended their line in three battalions, and sent 200 men forward as skirmishers – French buccaneers carrying first-class muskets, and all crack shots. These marched ahead, and the rest followed. Down from the hill came the buccaneers to where, on the open plain, the Spaniards awaited them.

Once the main body of rovers had reached the plain, the Spaniards gave a great shout of '*Viva el rey*' and sent their cavalry into the attack. But the horses, having to cross a swamp, made heavy going of it. As the Spaniards moved forward the 200 skirmishers made ready. Each man went down on one knee, and they fired by turns – one man aiming while his neighbour reloaded – so their fusillade never paused.

The Spaniards retaliated with a brisk volley, doing all they could to break through the line of buccaneers. Meanwhile the Spanish infantry, coming up in support of their cavalry, was held in check by the other body of buccaneers, and sharp fighting broke out. The Spaniards had planned to drive the wild bulls into the rear of the invading army and thereby break their formation, but while the rest of the buccaneers carried on with the fight, the men on the exposed rear rank turned to confront the bulls, waving their flags and firing a few shots into the herd. The wild beasts turned about and stampeded – the drovers running for their lives, like the cattle.

After two hours' hard fighting, the Spanish cavalry were thoroughly routed; most were dead or wounded, and the rest had fled. The Spanish foot-soldiers, seeing how little impression on the buccaneers their cavalry had made, and with no hope of winning by themselves, fired off their muskets, let them drop, and took to their heels.

Worn out with hunger and effort, the buccaneers had no strength for a pursuit. A few Spaniards who were unable to flee had hidden in the reeds by a stream, and these the buccaneers shot out of hand. Some grey friars, taken prisoner, were brought before Morgan, but he refused them a hearing and had them shot also. Then a cavalry captain, wounded in the battle, was brought in as prisoner. Morgan had him interrogated, and the captain gave him the details he wanted to know.

The enemy force had comprised 400 cavalry, twenty-four companies of foot, each 100 strong, and 600 Indians, besides a number of blacks and half-breeds, who had driven a total of 2,000 bulls in their attempt to break the buccaneers' line. The captain also said that at various points in the city there were gun emplacements, protected by mealsacks, to make a last-ditch resistance. Covering the road down which the buccaneers must advance was a redoubt with eight brass cannon, manned by fifty soldiers. On learning this, Morgan gave orders to change the line of march.

To the beat of drums his men fell in, and their casualties were reported. The buccaneers' losses proved to have been light, and there were but few wounded. Apart from dead and prisoners, all the Spaniards had by now disappeared. At least 600 Spaniards lay dead on the plain, in addition to the wounded who had managed to drag themselves off. The smallness of their own casualties raised the buccaneers' spirits enormously. After resting, they made ready for the attack on the city, taking an oath to stand by each other, shoulder to shoulder, and fight to the last man.

Having thus resolved, they marched on the city, taking their prisoners with them. The state of the city's defences was a surprise to them, after the morning's rout. Breastworks of mealsacks covered the main streets, each defended by batteries of cannon. The buccaneers attacked, but the guns, loaded with grapeshot, did them more damage than had the musketry fire of the Spaniards out on the plain, and the fighting was hard.

But the buccaneers shot everything dead that stood in their way, and in two hours the city was theirs. Though the Spaniards had sent all their valuables out of the city, there were many warehouses, stuffed with merchandise – silks, linen and other goods.

CHAPTER SIX

Morgan sends several ships marauding in the South Sea; the burning of Panama City and the plunder of the surrounding countryside; atrocities committed by the rovers; the return to Fort Chagre.

WHEN Morgan's buccaneers had taken complete possession of Panama City, he sent out twenty-five men in a barque which had been stranded at low tide in the harbour – for they have high and low water there, as in the English Channel. The harbour at high tide is so deep that a galleon can enter, but at low tide the sea is a mile off, leaving nothing but mud.

That noontide, Morgan secretly had houses in various parts set afire, but started a rumour that the Spaniards themselves had done this. By nightfall, most of the city was burning. Some tried to check the fire by blowing up houses, but in vain, for it was so well ablaze that once the flames reached a street, in half an hour it was on fire from end to end, and soon after in embers.

Most of the houses, including the finest, were of wood, usually cedar, and contained splendid paintings which the Spaniards had been unable to send away. There were seven monasteries and a convent, together with a hospital and cathedral and a parish church, embellished with wonderfully rich paintings and sculpture, though the monks had taken all the silver work away with them.

There were about 2,000 houses in the city belonging to prosperous merchants, and about 3,000 ordinary dwellings, together with stables for the pack animals which carried silver across country to the north coast. In the suburbs were orchards and gardens, full of fruit trees and vegetables. The Genoese had a big building there, used for their trade in Negro slaves, but this was burnt, along with the rest.

By next day, the whole city was reduced to ashes, as well as about 200 warehouses and the stables for the pack animals, which stood at a distance. All the animals within had been burnt, and so had many slaves who were hidden in the houses and had been unable to escape. The great piles of mealsacks inside the warehouses were still smouldering a month afterwards.

That night the buccaneers encamped round the city, in case the Spaniards came back, for they had been alarmed to find how greatly they were outnumbered. Next day, all the wounded were brought to the monastery church, still standing, which was made to serve as a guardhouse. All the guns were brought up and mounted around this church. Morgan drew up his men in battle order, to see once more what casualties had been sustained. About twenty men had been killed when putting the city to the sack, and as many wounded.

Morgan sent a detachment of 150 men, that same day, to take news of his victory to Fort Chagre. The main force of the buccaneers escorted this detachment out of the city. Several parties of Spaniards kept them under observation from a safe distance, but made off as fast as they could when the rovers showed signs of closing with them.

Towards noon, Morgan and his men once more entered the city and took up quarters wherever they could. One band of men went around searching the ruins of the burnt houses, where they found a fair amount of silverware and silver coins, which the Spaniards had hidden in their cisterns.

Next day two more parties, each of 150 men, went off to scour the countryside and discover where the citizens had hidden themselves. Two days later they came back, bringing with them 200 prisoners, men and women, including slaves. The same day saw the return of the barque Morgan had sent out, together with three captured vessels, but they had let their best prize slip through their fingers – a galleon, loaded with the King of Spain's silver, together with all the jewels and treasure of the foremost merchants in Panama. There were also nuns on board, taking their church ornaments and their silver and gold. This ship was armed with only seven cannon and a dozen muskets. Nor was it fully rigged even – it lacked topsails, and was moreover short of water.

The rovers learned all these facts when they captured a boat sent ashore from this galleon, with seven men in it, to fetch water. According to these men, the great ship could not possibly put to sea without water. But the buccaneer captain had been more inclined to sit drinking and sporting with a group of Spanish women he had taken prisoner, than to go at once in pursuit of the treasure ship.

Next day he did have the barque made ready to go and hunt down the galleon, but without success, for she had sailed away when the Spaniards aboard her found out that the buccaneers were at sea and had captured their ship's boat. Once they realized the galleon was out of reach, the men in the barque captured several boats laden with merchandise which they encountered near the islands of Tobago and Tobagilla, and then returned to Panama. On arrival they told Morgan what had happened.

The prisoners from the ship's boat, when questioned, said they knew well enough where the galleon was bound, but thought that reinforcements would have come aboard by now. At this news, Morgan had all the vessels in Panama harbour fitted out to give chase. Once more the buccaneers put to sea, this time in four barques with 120 men aboard. They were at sea for eight days, but in vain, for the great ship eluded them.

Since there was no hope of coming up with it, they decided to return once more to Tobago and Tobagilla, and there they came across a ship from Payta, laden with soap cloth, biscuit and sugar, and carrying some 20,000 pieces of eight. This ship they brought back to Panama, together with all the goods and prisoners they had taken in the islands.

The men Morgan had sent to Fort Chagre were back again, with good news. The garrison at Chagre had dispatched two

vessels to cruise the coast near the river estuary; they had
caught sight of a Spanish ship and had given chase. Since the
buccaneers in the fortress had run up the Spanish flag, the
fleeing ship, hard pressed, sought refuge in the river mouth.
Out of the frying-pan into the fire – for once the river was
reached, the Spaniards discovered they were under the guns
of their enemy. Most of the captured cargo was food, and the
buccaneers were well pleased, for the garrison had been on
short rations.

The news encouraged Morgan to stay longer in Panama,
and loot the province utterly. While some of his men went
marauding by sea, others scoured the countryside. A party of
200 men marched out each day, and as soon as one expedition
came back, another was ready to go out. From these sorties
they brought back considerable booty, and many prisoners,
whom day by day they made to suffer the greatest cruelties
and tortures, to make them disclose where their money had
been hidden.

One of their captives was a poor cripple whom they found
in a gentleman's house outside the city. This wretched man
had come across a good shirt in the house, and a pair of silk
breeches, which he had put on. A silver key was tied to the
points of these breeches. The buccaneers asked him about the
coffer which this key had been designed to fit. He had no
coffer, he told them, but had simply found the key in the
house.

When it became plain this was all he was going to tell them,
they strappado'd him until both his arms were entirely dis-
located, then knotted a cord so tight round the forehead that
his eyes bulged out, big as eggs. Since he still would not
admit where the coffer was, they hung him up by his male
parts, while one struck him, another sliced off his nose, yet
another an ear, and another scorched him with fire – tortures
as barbarous as man can devise. At last, when the wretch
could no longer speak and they could think of no new torments, they let a Negro stab him to death with a lance.

They committed many more such cruelties. They showed

little mercy, even to the monks, and would have shown none but for the hope of extracting money from them. Nor did they spare the women, except for those who yielded themselves completely. The rovers had a way of dealing with those women who held out. They would let them leave the church, which was being used as their prison, as if giving them a chance to go and wash themselves – but once a woman was in their hands they would work their will upon her, or beat her, starve her, or similarly torment her. Morgan, being the general, should have set a better example, but he was no better than the rest. Whenever a beautiful prisoner was brought in, he at once sought to dishonour her. Let me, while on this topic, tell of a woman so steadfast her name deserves to live.

The buccaneers, returning from sea, had brought prisoners with them from the islands of Tobago and Tobagilla, among others the young and very beautiful wife of a rich merchant. I shall not dwell on her beauty, more than to say that no lovelier woman could be found in all Europe. Her husband had gone to Peru on business, as is the custom in those parts, and, taking her valuables, this woman had fled with some of her friends.

The moment Morgan noticed her, he ordered them to put her apart from her friends, alone in a room with a female slave, though the lady wept and begged she might stay with those she knew. Morgan let her have everything she might need, and at mealtime sent her a dish or two from his own table, even though he had given her a slave girl to cook for her.

The woman at first put all this to Morgan's credit, and was much surprised, concluding that the buccaneers could not be so evil as she and many other Spanish women had supposed. When the Spanish army was about to leave the city to fight the invaders, some of the soldiers' wives had asked them to bring back a souvenir from the *ladrones*. Others, even more inquisitive, had wanted to watch the battle, from a safe distance. But the husbands had all refused, saying that the ladies would be terror-stricken – not at the fighting, but at the very sight of the buccaneers' deformity. These corsairs, they had said, are not like us, they are more like beasts – and even promised to bring back a few buccaneers' heads, to prove it.

Consequently many women, when first they actually saw the buccaneers, had cried out in amazement, '*Jesus, los ladrones son como los españoles*' – that is to say, 'Jesus, the robbers are just like us Spaniards!' This merchant's wife, deceived by Morgan's feigned civility, exclaimed, '*Los ladrones son tan corteses como si fueron espanoles*.' ('The robbers are as courteous as if they were Spanish.')

Each day Morgan took a stroll into the church where the prisoners were held, and made a point of looking in at the lattice of the room where this woman was kept apart. He would greet her, and sometimes even chat, for he spoke good Spanish. He also began to allow her friends to visit her. For three days this went on; then he sent a message, asking her to consent to her own dishonour, and afterwards made a similar demand directly, in person, giving her at the same time several precious jewels.

The lady, as chaste as she was well-bred, thanked him and admitted she was in his power, but said that from the first she had noticed his great personal courtesy towards her, which she hoped would not decrease. She found it hard to believe he had violent intentions, as it ill became a leader who wielded real power to make such demands on one whose life was in his hands.

These civil words could not cool Morgan's inflamed lust. He besought her all the more vehemently, promising to give her back the value of all she had lost, in the form of jewels. She for her part used every turn of phrase she could think of, but Morgan would not leave her in peace. So persistently did he badger her that at last she felt obliged to tell him he would have to let her soul go free before he could work his will on her body, since she would never give in so long as she lived. After telling him this she kept silent and would say no more.

This woman's refusal so enraged Morgan that finally he had

her locked up in another room, alone, and forbade the others to go near her. Her clothes were taken away, and each day she was given so little to eat she was almost dying with hunger. Yet this did not weaken her resolve; every day she prayed to God that if it so pleased him to inflict this punishment upon her, he would yet give her the strength to resist Morgan's violence.

Morgan had this woman tormented in this way on the pretext that she had been in touch with the Spaniards, and had sent out a slave with several letters. I would never have believed a woman could be so steadfast, had I not myself seen her and spoken with her. Once or twice I helped by bringing her food, though this had to be done on the sly. Later in my narrative I shall speak once more of this woman, telling how misfortune dogged her, not only amidst enemies, but also when with her friends.

After three weeks in Panama – three weeks of plundering, both by land and sea – Morgan began to get ready for moving out. Each company had to collect a given number of mules, to carry the booty as far as the river, about eight leagues away. Meanwhile, some hundred of his men agreed among themselves to leave Morgan in the lurch, take the ship which lay in the harbour, and raid the South Sea. They intended to capture a big ship, load it with their plunder, and get back to Europe by way of the East Indies.

With this plan in mind, they had stowed away in a hiding-place all kinds of necessary stores, such as gunpowder, bullets, meal and biscuit – even several cannon, with which they planned to fortify an anchorage at one or other of the islands, to use as their base. Their scheme might have succeeded, had not one among them told Morgan all about it.

He at once gave orders to have the masts of their ship cut off and burnt, together with the masts of all the other boats in the harbour, and this frustrated their plan. Meanwhile the mules were being collected, and Morgan sent off some of the Spaniards to fetch ransom money for their wives, children and slaves, as well as a few of the monks, to fetch ransom both for themselves and for the other monks who remained behind as hostages.

Morgan then had all the cannon spiked and their trunnions broken off. Before his departure he sent scouts to find what the president of Panama was doing, for some of the prisoners had said he was getting men together and planning ambushes to bar the rovers' path. But the scouts came back and told Morgan they had come across no signs of ambush, and they also brought along several new prisoners, who said that though the president had wished to form a new striking force, his men had deserted and his plans had come to nothing.

On 24 February 1671, Morgan left Panama City with all his men, and 175 mules laden with silver plate and coin, as well as with five or six hundred prisoners – men, women, children and slaves. That first day they travelled about a league from the city, halting in an open field beside the river. There the buccaneer army encamped in a circle, with the prisoners in the middle.

All night long you could hear nothing but the moaning and crying of all the women and the many little children, who knew no better than that the rovers would carry them off to their own country. One cried out for his father, another for his friends, while a third called on his fatherland. Worst of all, these poor folk were suffering great hunger and thirst. It was pitiful to see the many poor women with babies at their breast and nothing to feed the poor little mites. They begged Morgan on their bare knees to let them go, but the moans of all these wretched people were not enough to move him to any compassion. He told them he had not come to listen to their groans, but to get money, and they would never get out of his clutches without it. That was all the comfort these poor souls could get out of Morgan.

Next morning they were on the march again, and the weeping and wailing began afresh. One party of buccaneers marched in front, the prisoners were in the middle, and the rest of the rovers brought up the rear. The woman of whom we have spoken was made to march by herself between two buccaneers, suffering great discomfort from the heat of the sun and the difficulty of the path – as did many of the ladies, not being accustomed to such hardship. But Morgan did not prevent his men from giving a helping hand to the women, with the single exception of this unfortunate lady. (I call her unfortunate, and not without reason, for it seemed that ill-luck followed her everywhere.)

She had instructed some monks of her acquaintance, whom she trusted, to fetch money from a certain place to pay her ransom. Instead of using it for this purpose, they released some of their brethren with the luckless woman's money. If the truth had not been revealed by a slave, who was bringing her a letter, Morgan would have carried her off to Jamaica. However, when the buccaneers saw for themselves that the money really was for the lady's ransom, they let her go and seized the monks.

On arrival at the village of Cruz, on the bank of the river Chagre, Morgan informed all the prisoners that their ransom money must be produced within three days, or else he would carry them off. Meanwhile, he had all the rice and maize in the vicinity collected to provision the ships, and some of the prisoners secured their release. He moved out of Cruz on 15 March with all his plunder and those prisoners who had still not paid their ransom. These included the monks who had purloined the money of the merchant's wife, but they were barely half-way to Chagre when money arrived to set these men free.

At this point Morgan gathered all his men together and reminded them of their old custom of swearing an oath that they had not kept back for themselves so much as six penny-worth, whether of silver, gold, ambergris, diamonds, pearls or other precious stones. There had been some examples, he said, of fellows who had sworn a false oath. Therefore, to prevent any such occurrence, he had decided not to exact an oath from anybody – but to have a general search made, without any exceptions. This met with the hearty approval of Morgan's cronies among the captains, whom he had already told of his intentions. One man was chosen from each company to do the searching. Morgan, for the look of the thing, allowed himself to be searched, as did all the captains, so that no one escaped.

The French buccaneers murmured against such a procedure, but they were in a minority and so had to keep quiet. If the rovers had known Morgan had had this idea in mind, they would not have brought along everything they'd found.

After all had been searched, they embarked in the canoes and other vessels waiting in the river, and on 19 March arrived at Fort Chagre. Everything was still going well there, apart from the fact that most of the wounded men they had left there had died of hunger. Those in sound health had had a hard enough time of it. They had been forced to eat those birds the Spaniards call *gallinazos*, or buzzards, which live only on carrion. Great multitudes had been found picking the corpses of the fallen Spaniards.

These birds look like turkeys and are about the same size: the first time I saw some, I shot a couple, thinking they were turkeys. Buzzards are great devourers of flesh; four of them will eat up a whole ox or a horse in a day. As fast as they eat, they get rid of it again at the other end. They are extremely timid, and dare not attack any living creature, however small, while it is capable of any movement. Their beaks cannot pierce an animal's hide, so first they peck out the eyes and make a hole, and then laboriously creep into the belly of the carcass and eat it up from the inside, leaving dry skin and bones and the flesh all gone.

They do great damage among the cattle in the fields, for when a cow or a mare has given birth, and the young one is still too weak to move, down they swoop and peck out its eyes. Whole flocks of them used to follow the hunters, just as they now followed the buccaneers in Panama – for no expedition set out but resulted in pickings for the buzzards, either men or animals. Their presence warned the Spaniards of the approach of the rovers: when they saw a flock of these birds in the sky, they would say to each other, 'The corsairs are coming.'

Buzzards are found throughout the continent, and even on some of the islands, such as Cuba and Jamaica. Some say there used to be multitudes of them on Hispaniola, but they were driven away by witchcraft. Mostly they are to be found around or even in the towns, and they scavenge all the refuse that is thrown away. You can always see them perched up on houses and churches, on the alert for anything that falls. The moment a bit of meat or anything else is thrown out of a house, ten or a score of them come swooping down on it.

They are capable of fasting for a long time; according to people who have studied the matter, buzzards can exist a whole month without food. The buccaneers who had been left in Fort Chagre said that when the birds first flew down to pick the corpses they were so thin there wasn't a couple of ounces of flesh on their whole body – but after a fortnight's feasting, they were as heavy as turkeys. I include this information because we have no such birds in Europe.

When Morgan and his men had arrived at Chagre, he thought it advisable to have the booty shared out promptly as food was so scarce. This was agreed, and they also approved Morgan's proposal of sending a vessel to Porto Bello, to set the prisoners from St Catalina ashore and also to demand a ransom for Fort Chagre. Two days later the sloop returned, with the news that the Spaniards refused to pay any ransom at all.

The following day each company received its share of the plunder – or as much at least as Morgan vouchsafed them. When it was dealt out individually, each man found his share came to no more than 200 pieces of eight. The wrought silver was reckoned at only ten pieces of eight the pound; the price offered in exchange for various jewels was dirt cheap, and many jewels were missing – for which Morgan was publicly accused by the buccaneers.

When he saw the common folk had begun to grumble so bitterly, Morgan instantly made ready to leave. He had the fortress demolished and set on fire, after he'd had the brass cannon removed to his ship. Then he immediately set sail, without any signal of departure: let those follow him who chose. In fact he was followed by only three or four ships, those of his cronies, who (according to the rovers) had split the loot with him.

Three or four of the French buccaneer ships gave chase, and had a mind to attack if they could outsail him. But Morgan's ship was well stocked with victuals and he could keep to his course. Not so the others: one dropped off here, another there, to look for food and get hold of enough provisions to enable them to return to Jamaica.

CHAPTER SEVEN

The author's voyage along the coast of Costa Rica.

AFTER parting from Morgan, we continued our voyage along the coast of Costa Rica, looking for a place where we could obtain food supplies and also caulk our vessel, which had become leaky and foul. In a few days we entered a large bay called Boca del Toro, a very good place for cutting reeds and catching turtles. This bay is about ten leagues in circumference, and is sheltered from every wind by numerous off-shore islands. Around the bay live various Indian tribes, whom the Spaniards have been unable to bring to submission. These tribes of *Indios bravos* cannot understand each other's speech, and are constantly at war.

At the eastern corner of the bay live Indians who formerly used to like trading with the buccaneers. They would bring them everything they had – maize, cassava and fruits of all kinds, even hens and pigs and other animals. In exchange, the rovers would give them old ironwork, pieces of coral and suchlike things which these people wear for adornment. The place was always a bolt-hole for the rovers when they needed a refuge, but on one occasion they treated the Indians so badly that now no buccaneer dare come ashore there. They carried off the women and killed some of the men, and since that time the Indians will have no dealings with them.

On entering the bay, we went at once to a place where we hoped to catch game of some sort, but we found nothing, and had to be satisfied with the crocodiles' eggs we found buried in the sand. We sailed to the east of the bay, where we found three of our comrades' ships, like ourselves formerly part of Morgan's squadron. They had come with the same intentions, but had fared so badly they'd had to put themselves on rations, eating only once a day, while their ships were being careened so they could leave again.

When we saw how matters stood, we left at once and sailed to the western part, where we made a reasonably good catch of turtle, enough for us to live on. After some time there we began to run short of water – not because none was to be had, but because we dared not go and fetch it on account of the Indians. Yet in the end necessity drove us to go to a river to fetch water. Every man went on the expedition; one party ranged the forest, while the other filled the casks.

Scarcely an hour after our landing our comrades at the river were surprised by a band of Indians, who tried to prevent them from getting the water. As soon as we heard the cry '*Aux armes!*' we rushed through the forest with guns blazing, although we could see nobody until the end, when we glimpsed a group of Indians running through the trees. We pursued them, firing all the time, but they all got away except two who lay dead.

From his attire, one of the dead Indians seemed to have been a person of consequence. He wore a loincloth made from tree-bark, beaten soft as silk between two stones. He also wore a gold beard – a thin gold plate as wide as three fingers and about six inches long, weighing about as much as three lead bullets. This was attached to his underlip by a thread passing through two little holes. The other man was stark naked, but he had a beard of tortoiseshell.

Their weapons were nothing but staves of palm trees, about seven feet long, sharpened at both ends and barbed at one. Both points had been hardened in fire. We searched for their dwellings but could find none, from which we concluded they must live deep in the forest. We would very much have liked to have taken one of these people alive, to try and get on friendly terms with the tribe and trade for food, but they were too wild for there to be any chance of this.

Despite this encounter, we drew as much water as we needed from the river and then left for our ships. That night we heard a great outcry from the Indians on the shore, from which we guessed that more of the tribe had gathered and were lamenting the death of their comrades with shrieks and wails. They had no boats or canoes, as far as we could see.

As we could do no good in this place and were unable to catch more than we needed for our daily food, we decided to set sail and make for Jamaica. We beat against the wind as far as the mouth of the river Chagre, when we saw a ship bearing down on us, giving us chase. We supposed it to be a Spanish ship come from Cartagena bringing men to occupy Fort Chagre, so we ran before the wind with all sails set. But the stranger sailed faster than we did, and after a pursuit of twenty-four hours overtook us. When we were close by each other, we saw it was a ship of our comrades. They had been trying to make for Nombre de Dios and thence to Cartagena, seeking their fortune, but since wind and currents were contrary had decided to return to Boca del Toro.

This pursuit had done us a great deal of harm, for we had lost more distance in two days than we had gained in a fortnight, so we too were obliged to return to our old place, but did not stay there long. We sailed farther to a bay called Boca del Drago, intending to catch a certain aquatic animal which the Spanish call *manati* and the Dutch call the sea-cow, because it has a nose, mouth and teeth like a cow's. These animals always live in the water, near places where the seabed is covered with grass, on which they feed.

Their shape is remarkable: the head is like a cow's, but without ears – only a tiny little hole on each side, into which you can scarcely stick your little finger. They have two wings or fins on the neck, like those of a shark but somewhat longer, with three claws at the end, and below them two udders. The whole body is smooth right down to the tail, which is flat and rounded at the end, and is three to four feet broad when the animal is full-grown. The largest of these creatures measures about twenty-four feet long.

The skin is hairy and thick, being a good three inches thick on the back. When dry it is as stiff as whalebone and can be used for making walking-sticks. Under the belly, the skin is thinner and more supple. The internal organs – liver, lungs, intestines, stomach, kidneys and all – are just like those of the ox. They have sixteen ribs on each side, rounded and fairly thick in the middle and very hard at each end. When they copulate, they clasp each other belly to belly. The male has a penis like a bull's and the female organ is below the navel and like a cow's. The manatee bears but one calf at a time, but I cannot say how long she gestates, for I have had no opportunity of observing this.

These creatures have remarkably acute hearing, and if one makes the slightest noise it is impossible to catch them. For this reason those who hunt them do not use ordinary oars to row their boats, but certain short bladed paddles, which the Indians call *pagayos* and the Spaniards *canaletes*, with which they can move along softly and soundlessly. The canoeists dare not speak a word, but follow signals from the harpoonist who stands in the prow. The manatees are harpooned in the same manner as turtles, but with a rather longer spear with hooks on the end. They have very small eyes and can see little – just the opposite of the turtles, which have wonderfully sharp eyes but are deaf.

The flesh looks like veal, but tastes like pork and has plenty of fat. The flesh is salted and smoked, in the same way as the *boucaniers* prepare their meat. A large manatee will yield a good two tons of meat, not counting the bones and the fat. The tail is all fat, which the rovers melt down and pour into earthenware pots. They eat it with maize, which they cook like groats. The fat does not impart a fishy taste, but in fact is much better than cooking-oil or lard. This is all I can tell you of these animals, for I have discovered nothing further about them.

Having arrived at the bay, we caught as many of these manatees as we could. We salted the flesh and used up the offal and the meat left on the bones for our daily fare. One day, having caught nothing and not wishing to broach our supply of salt meat, we decided to go fishing and shooting birds at a near-by island. After a while we noticed an Indian canoe, with four men aboard. As soon as the men caught sight of us, they made back for the shore with all speed. We promptly gave chase, to see whether there was any chance of trading with them for foodstuffs.

But these Indians will have no dealings with Christians. They beached their canoe and, as soon as they had jumped ashore, picked up their boat and ran away. We pursued them so hotly they were forced to abandon the canoe, which nevertheless the four of them had managed to carry 200 paces into the forest. This canoe weighed at least a ton, so that we were amazed at the men's strength – we had enough to do, the eleven of us, to carry it back again to the water.

When the Indians saw us carrying off their canoe, they started screaming at the tops of their voices. We fired at the places where the voices came from, but to what effect we could not tell. We dared not go far into the woods, there are so many Indians on this islet.

Our pilot, who had directed our course and who had been in these parts several times before, told us that once he came there with a whole fleet of buccaneer ships. Some of the men took the canoes close inshore to do some fishing and look out for birds to shoot. Several Indians had climbed up into the trees by the water's edge, and, as the canoes came close by, they leapt down and with great agility seized some of the buccaneers and had carried them off into the forest before the rest of their comrades were able to do anything to help. On the following day the admiral landed with 500 men to rescue the abducted buccaneers, but they had barely set foot on shore when the Indians forced them to retire with all speed.

If such a force had been unable to prevail against the Indians, we judged that we should be able to hold our own still less, so we left the place as soon as possible. We found nothing in the captured canoe but a net – four fathoms long and half a fathom broad – and four staves, about seven feet long, made of palm wood. These we supposed to be their weapons. One end was pointed, and at the other were seven or eight barbs, as may be seen from the sketch overleaf.

The canoe was of cedar wood, and so clumsily made that we guessed they had no iron tools. The islet where these Indians live is very small – scarcely three leagues in circumference, in fact. They have no other place to live, for they are at war with the Indians on the mainland coast, nor can the tribes understand each other. As for us, we too dared not land on the mainland, for there too the Indians will have dealings with nobody.

In my opinion, the reason why the Indians shun all contact with strangers is that when the Spaniards first came to this country they subjected the inhabitants to such cruelty they looked on the conquerors with terror, and fled into the interior. Here they live in the wilderness, without cultivating the land, living only on fish from the river and fruit from the trees. After their experiences they dare trust no white men, looking on them all as Spaniards. Indeed, they could not trust the other Indians even, for some tribes had taken sides with the Spanish, and cruelly tormented their fellow-countrymen.

Having thus fled into different regions, their manner of speech changed and this led to enmity. For nothing brings about more enmity between two peoples than their being unable to understand each other – for it is impossible for an ordinary man to love or esteem someone if he cannot understand him. For this reason these savage tribes make war against each other – not because one claims what the other has, or because one has deprived the other of land or honour, or on account of any debts – but simply because they do not understand each other. When they have carried off any prisoners, they subject them to the most horrible torments in the world and then use them as slaves. These are my observations on the savage tribes in the bay of Boca del Drago.

At last we decided to leave this bay, as we could see no way of obtaining provisions, finding it difficult enough to get as much food as we needed from day to day. We sailed westwards along the coast, and after a journey of twenty-four hours reached a place called Rio de Zeura, where the Spaniards from Cartagena have a few houses. We had intended to catch turtles there, for it was the season when they come ashore to lay eggs, but we did not find any. Then we thought of paying the Spaniards a visit, but these folk had left us nothing but empty houses, having fled into the woods as soon as they saw us coming. We had to content ourselves with bananas, or *platanos* as the Spaniards call them, which I shall not describe as they are well known to everyone who has been in the west.

We loaded our boat with these fruit and then sailed along the coast looking for a good harbour where we could careen. Our vessel was very leaky, and we had to keep some of the slaves continuously at work on the pump or we should have sunk. The water was pouring in as fast as we could pump it out.

After fourteen days cruising along the coast we came to a large bay known as Bleeckveldt Bay, after a buccaneer who used to put in there very often, to repair his ship. This was an excellent place for careening, and we set to work as quickly as possible. While some of our men were busy on the ship, the others went hunting in the forest. In these woods are wild pigs which have their navels on their backs, and are called navel pigs on this account; there are also badgers, but not many. We met with few wild boar or badgers, so most of our hunting consisted of shooting monkeys and pheasants for our daily food – mostly monkeys, which are found in great numbers.

Although we were in a wretched state for want of fresh food, we did not take much pleasure in shooting the monkeys, for out of every fifteen or sixteen that we hit, we scarcely got three or four. Unless they were shot stone dead it was impossible to get hold of them, for they would cling by the tail to the tips of thin branches until they died, and even then, hang there until they rotted. The females carry their young on their back like the Negro women carry their babies. If the mother was shot dead and the young monkey remained alive, it would not leave its mother, whether she fell or not, but stay clinging tight to her back.

When anyone passes under a tree full of monkeys, they will spatter him with excrement and break off branches and throw them at his head. When a troop of monkeys has been fired on and one of them is hit, the others immediately gather round and sniff the wound. If there is much blood spurting out, some of them squeeze the wound to check the blood, others get moss from the trees and stick it in the place, while still others fetch certain herbs, which they chew and then press in the wound. I have often observed with great wonder the way these animals stand by each other in time of need and endeavour to help their fellows, though in peril of their lives.

These monkeys are tasty and very nourishing; every day we boiled and roasted so much monkey-flesh we became used to it, and to us it tasted better than pheasant. We lived in this manner about eight days – some of us caulking the ship, others cleaning and refitting her, and the rest out hunting. We had several slaves, men and women, with us, and these we also set to work. The men chopped firewood and burned lime, which we used instead of tar for smearing the ship and making her watertight. The women fetched water from some wells we had dug on the shore.

The ship was nearly ready, and the women were sent to fill up the water-casks with all speed. At break of day they went with their pots to the wells, two of the girls walking some way behind the others, plucking fruit from the trees to eat. Suddenly, they heard from the wood the shrieks of their companions. Thinking some creature had bitten them, the girls ran forward to help, but before they reached the spot they saw a band of Indians coming out of the wood. Instantly they dropped their pots and began to run, screaming, '*Indios! Indios!*'

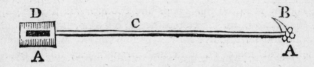

A. A piece of pyrites, fastened to the arrow
B. A wooden barb, similarly attached
C. The arrow
D. The case at the end of the arrow

We immediately seized our guns and rushed to the place where the girls said they had seen the Indians. Here we found the dead bodies of the two Negro women, each stuck with twelve or thirteen arrows; they had been shot through the body, the neck and the legs. It seemed as if the savages had taken delight in transfixing them with arrows, for the first one alone would have been sufficient to kill them.

These arrows were of a remarkable design; they were made of staves about eight feet long and as thick as a finger. At one end was a wooden barb, spliced on with string, and a piece of pyrites or fire-stone, similarly attached. At the other end was a sort of small wooden case, containing a few small stones, which rattled a little as the arrow moved. Some of the arrows were made of palm wood, painted red, and shining as bright as lacquer. We supposed that such weapons would have belonged to the chiefs, and we noticed that these were the arrows which had been plunged in the middle of the dead girls' bodies.

These arrows are made without any iron tools whatever. Everything the Indians make, they first burn the wood away as far as required, and then scrape it with flints.

These Indians move through the forest swiftly and silently. However narrowly we searched, we could never find their footprints nor the slightest sign of their passing. They were so cautious they had put leaves between the little stones in the boxes at the end of their arrows, to stop the rattle.

Having searched the woods and tried in vain to find any canoe or raft of theirs, we returned to our ship, embarked our goods and set sail. We no longer felt safe on shore, fearing the Indians might come in such strength they might overpower us completely.

CHAPTER EIGHT

The author arrives at Cabo Gracias a Dios;
trade with the Indians there; their manner of life.
Arrival at Isla de los Pinos and return to
Jamaica.

THE death of our women slaves at the hands of the Indians
had put such fear in us we got out of that place as fast as
possible. We set our course for Cabo Gracias a Dios, where
we hoped to find the comfort we needed – a safe refuge and
the chance of obtaining provisions, for the Indians who live
there trade with the buccaneers and treat them well.

After six days we arrived at this cape. Its name means
'Thanks be to God' – and so said we, as a man who has been
in great danger of drowning cries when he is taken out of the
water, 'Thanks be to God, for he has saved me.' We thanked
God that he had delivered us in our great need, and had let
us come to a place where we could enjoy the friendship of the
inhabitants and supply our wants.

As we dropped anchor we saw two Christians on the beach,
who waited to welcome us. The rovers are on such friendly
terms with the native people they can stay and live among
them without risk of harm, and without a care in the world.
The Indians give them all they need, in exchange for which
they give the Indians nothing but old knives, axes and tools
of that sort.

When a rover comes there, he buys a woman from the
Indians for an old axe or knife, and for this fee she must stay
with him till he leaves. Should he come back again in three
or four years' time, this same woman must return to him. A
man who has taken an Indian wife has nothing to worry
about: she brings him his daily food, as is customary among
the Indians. The man need do nothing but a little hunting or

fishing. A white man need not even do this, but may order an Indian to do it for him.

The Indians often go to sea with the rovers, and may spend three or four years away without visiting their homeland, so among them are men who can speak very good English and French – just as there are many buccaneers who speak the Indian language well. These Indians are a great asset to the rovers, as they are very good harpoonists, extremely skilful in spearing turtles, manatees and fish. In fact, an Indian is capable of keeping a whole ship's company of 100 men supplied with food, when he is in a place where there's something to catch.

When we landed at the cape, the Indians came to meet us with all kinds of fruit, and looked to see if there were any of their acquaintance among us. Two of our party could speak their language well, having lived there a long time. We stayed among these people for some time, so I had the opportunity of studying their lives and customs, which I will briefly relate here.

These Indians form a little republic, having no chief over them whom they acknowledge as lord or king. The land they possess is some thirty leagues in circumference. They have no friendship with their neighbours, and none at all with the Spaniards, who are great enemies of theirs. They are few in number, not more than fifteen or sixteen hundred. Among them are some Negroes whom they keep as slaves. These people had seized control of a ship and were endeavouring to escape in it when they ran the vessel aground near the cape, and the Indians promptly made them all slaves again.

The Indians are divided into two communities, or provinces as we might say. One community lives inland, where they have plantations, and the other lives by the seashore. The former are more inclined to labour than the seashore folk, who are too lazy even to build themselves houses. When it rains, their only protection is a palm leaf, which they turn to face the wind so that the leaf keeps off the driving rain. Their clothing consists of nothing but a loincloth to cover their nakedness. Some are made of tree-bark, beaten between stones and made soft, which is also used for sleeping-mats, and others are made of cotton. Their weapon is the spear, tipped with iron or with shark's teeth.

They have some notion of almighty God, yet do not practise any form of religion; I have never observed any act of worship. Unlike many Indians in America, they do not believe in the devil, nor are they so tormented by him as are other tribes.

Their food consists mainly of fruits, such as bananas, plantains, pineapples, sweet potatoes and cassava, as well as crabs and fish which they catch by spearing. They make all sorts of delicious drinks. The most common is called *achioc*, and is made from the fruits of a certain palm, which are crushed in hot water. They leave it to stand a little, and drink the liquor when it has settled. It has a pleasant taste and is very nourishing.

Another drink is made from ripe bananas, which are roasted in hot ashes and then plunged, hot from the fire, into water and kneaded by hand until the mixture becomes thick as porridge – thus supplying food and drink at the same time. Bananas are also used to make a strong wine. For this, the ripe fruits are kneaded in cold water inside huge calabashes which grow in those parts. The liquor is left to ferment for eight days, when it becomes as strong as Spanish wine. The Indians invite their friends to enjoy this drink.

Yet another drink, even more delicious, is made by taking pineapples, roasting them till half done and kneading them in the same way as the bananas. When well mixed, they add a third part of wild honey and let all ferment together. The liquor looks just the colour of Spanish wine and is most delectable.

Their drinks are the best things they have, for they know nothing about preparing and cooking food. Yet they have a very pleasant way of holding feasts and entertaining their friends. When an Indian has made some wine, he invites his friends round to try it. At the time he expects his guests to arrive, he combs his hair, smears it with palm-oil and paints himself black all over. His wife combs her hair, and she paints herself entirely red.

Then the man takes his weapons – three or four spears – and walks about 300 paces along the road he expects his friends to come by. When he sees them approaching, the man falls flat on his face at their feet and lies as still as if he were dead. The friends help him up and take him to his house. The host goes in first, and all his guests fall down on their faces outside, just as he did. One by one, he helps them to their feet and brings them in his home. The women, however, do not honour each other with any ceremonies, as far as I have noticed.

When the friends are all inside, each is presented with a calabash full of the thick gruel of roasted bananas. These calabashes hold about half a gallon, and they must eat and drink it all up. Then the host takes away the empty gourds, and makes his guests a speech of welcome. After this, they drink the liquor they have been invited to sample, without eating anything except some fruit.

As they get drunk, they sing and dance, and give their women many caresses and, to demonstrate their amorous feelings, take their spears and stab their male parts, in the presence of the women. I had often heard the buccaneers tell of this custom, but would not believe it – until later on I saw it for myself. They do the same sort of thing when courting a woman, to show her how much they love her. Sometimes fights break out when the men are drunk, and occasionally they stab each other to death – but this happens seldom.

They keep up various ceremonies to do with marriage. An Indian may not marry a girl without the consent of her parents and friends. A suitor is asked by the father whether he can hunt well and fish well, make good spears and harpoons and rope. If his answers are satisfactory, the father takes a small calabash of liquor from which he drinks, then passes it to the young man, who drinks and then gives it to the bride. Usually when anyone is offered a calabash of liquor he is supposed to drink it all up, but in this case all three share it, as a sign of their blood-friendship.

Similar ceremonies take place when a buccaneer takes up with an Indian girl, but instead of being questioned by her father, he has to present him with a knife and an axe. When the rover goes away, he brings the woman back to her father – with no ill feelings on either side. This will not hinder an Indian from later taking her to wife, but once married, her husband will keep her to himself.

These people make no ceremony over the birth of a child, as the Carib Indians do. As soon as a woman has given birth, she gets up and washes the baby in the river or some other water, and then swaddles it in one of her loincloths, or *cabalas*, as they are called. How she is able to do so, I leave it to the ladies to judge, who have more experience of these matters.

These Indians also have some strange customs to do with the dead. When her husband dies, his wife must bury him herself, with all his loincloths, spears, fishing-tackle and all the jewels he used to wear in his ears and round his neck. Every day she has to bring food and drink to his grave. Each morning she brings plantains and a calabash of liquor, and if birds come and peck at the offering, this is considered a good sign. This goes on for a whole year. They calculate the time by the moon, reckoning fifteen for a year.

Some writers assert that the food the Indians take to their dead is carried off by the devil, but I do not consider this to be true. I have often helped myself to these offerings, as the fruit they put on the graves is always the ripest and most delicious they can find.

When a year (according to their reckoning) has passed, the woman goes and opens up the grave, and takes up all the bones she finds under the earth. She washes them and leaves them in the sun to dry. Then she wraps them up in a *cabala*, and has to carry them on her back for as long as they were under the ground. For fifteen months she sleeps with them, works with them, carries the bones around with her everywhere. When the time is up, she hangs them in front of her hut, if she has one, or in front of the house of her nearest friend.

According to their laws, the widow cannot marry again until the two years are gone by – the year under the earth and the year of carrying the bones. When a buccaneer married to an Indian woman dies, she performs the ceremonies just as if he had been an Indian. A man does not carry the bones of his dead wife. Men who were enslaved at the time of their death do not have their bones carried, but food-offerings are brought to their graves. Any prisoners of war they capture are made into slaves. The Negroes who live among the Indians carry out their customs in all things.

These people are subject to the same illnesses as white men, such as dysentery and smallpox. When they have a fever, they go and lie in the water until the fever is passed. When a sickness comes among them, many die.

These are the observations I was able to make during my stay. When we were refreshed and the Indians had given us all they could, we left the place and steered for Cuba, and in fourteen days reached Isla de los Pinos, which lies to the south of that island. We had to put into harbour to refit our vessel, which we could no longer keep above water.

On arrival, two Indians we had brought with us from Cabo Gracias a Dios went out fishing, and some of us went hunting, for the island is full of cattle, which the Spaniards brought there to breed. We'd hardly been there four hours before we had caught enough to feed 2,000 – cattle, turtles, manatees and fish of all kinds. Then all the discomforts we had suffered were forgotten. Now we called each other nothing but brothers – but then, when we were short of food, if we passed within half a dozen yards we were in each other's way.

We had a good opportunity of careening our ship, for we had no enemies to watch out for, except the Spaniards – but we were not afraid of them: we sought them out more than they did us. Still, we had to keep a good look-out at night for crocodiles, which are very numerous. When hungry, they are not scared of anybody – as was proved to us by what happened to one of our company.

He went into the woods accompanied by a Negro, and trod unawares on a crocodile which lay hidden at the edge of a pool. The crocodile seized him by the leg and began to pull him down. This man was brave and strong, however; he drew his knife and defended himself so furiously that he killed the crocodile, although he then collapsed, faint from loss of blood. His slave, who had fled, came back and helped him along until they were about a league from the shore. We carried him the rest of the way in a hammock.

After that, none of us dared to go alone into the woods. We went out in groups of ten or a dozen every day, especially to kill crocodiles. At night they would try to get into our ship, scrabbling with their fore-feet on the ship's timbers as if to climb up. We used to noose a rope round their necks and hoist them inboard.

When we were well supplied with provisions and had done some repairs to our ship, we continued our journey to Jamaica. On arrival there, we found that a third of our fleet had still not come in to port.

Morgan had plans of mounting another expedition to go and take possession of St Catalina, as the garrison had been withdrawn. He was prevented from putting his ideas into action by the arrival of an English man-of-war, with orders from the King recalling the governor of Jamaica to England to account for all the injuries the buccaneers of Jamaica had done to the Spaniards. A new governor arrived on the same ship. Morgan himself also went back to England on the return voyage.

The new governor promptly sent ships to all the Spanish ports with assurances of good fellowship and promises that no more buccaneers should sail out from Jamaica. At the same time, with the excuse of these public protestations of peace, the governor managed to carry on a brisk trade with the Spaniards, using a group of Jews who lived on Jamaica as his agents, to conceal his negotiations.

On hearing this news, some of the buccaneers who had not yet come into port decided not to put in an appearance, but stayed at sea taking all the plunder they could. Later on they took a town called Villa de los Cayos, on the north side of Cuba, where they committed their usual cruel and godless acts.

However, the new governor succeeded in arresting a few of these rovers, and had them hanged. When they learned of this, the others fled to join the French on Tortuga, where they live to this day – for they are so accustomed to the buccaneering life it is impossible for them to give it up. If one port is forbidden them, then they sail to another, for this part of the world is full of fair harbours, where the buccaneers can find all they need to maintain their ships, and food in abundance.

CHAPTER NINE

M. Bertrand d'Ogeron, governor of Tortuga, is shipwrecked and falls into the hands of the Spaniards; his escape, and attempt to liberate the rest of his men.

IN 1673, when France and Holland were at war, forces were assembled in the French islands to attack and destroy the Dutch possessions in the West Indies. The French general issued commissions in the name of the King to all ships willing to be employed in the destruction of the enemy. He himself had formed a fleet both of men-of-war and merchant ships, summoned from all quarters and gathered together to assault the island of Curaçao. M. Bertrand d'Ogeron, governor of Tortuga, embarked on a ship of war with four or five hundred buccaneers from Hispaniola, with the intention of joining the fleet in the attack on Curaçao. But this design came to nothing, on account of a disaster which befell him on the south side of the island of Puerto Rico. A violent storm rose in the night and drove his ship on the rocks near the Guadanillas islands, and it soon broke in pieces. M. d'Ogeron and his men had to make for the shore to save their lives.

The Spaniards of Puerto Rico thought they must have come to plunder the island (as the French had often done before) so they gathered together a suitable force and at day-break went to the place where the sailors were. The latter, who were in a wretched state, felt far more inclined to ask for quarter than to fight. All they'd managed to save was their own lives and the clothes they stood up in, a shirt and linen trousers. But down the Spaniards came on them, with all the men they had been able to amass – Negroes and Indians and half-breeds, but not many white men.

When the French saw them coming, they went to meet them to beg for quarter, pleading that they were Europeans come to trade in the French islands, who had had the ill-luck to have their ship broken up on the rocks in the gale. All the answer their lamentations and pleas for mercy received was, '*Ha, perros ladrones, no hay cuartel para vosotros!*' With these words, which mean, 'You thieving dogs, there's no quarter for you!' the Spanish forces flung themselves upon the French, killing many of them.

However, when the Spaniards saw the French made no resistance, not even having a weapon to fight with, they left off their slaughter, although still convinced the French had come to plunder the island. They bound the survivors together in twos and threes and marched them from the shore to the savana. Here the Spaniards asked what had become of their leader, and the prisoners all replied that he had drowned, although this was not true. M. d'Ogeron himself had begged his men to say this, before the Spaniards had closed with them. The Spaniards did not believe he was dead, and put some of the Frenchmen to the rack to make them say who was their leader. Some of them, unable to endure the pain, died under this torture.

D'Ogeron acted as though he were a simpleton, unable to speak properly, so the Spaniards let him loose, without doing him any injury. They even gave him something to eat, while the others went hungry. The prisoners were given too little to live without misery, and too much to allow them to die of hunger. If any man fell sick the Spaniards used him for their cruel diversion before he died. They would hold a tournament, with the victim tied to a tree, riding down on him with poised lances to see whose aim was best.

M. d'Ogeron, who was a man of good intellect though he feigned to be a fool, resolved to risk his life to set his men free, when he saw the barbarity with which they were treated. As well as being guarded, the French prisoners were in bonds – all except d'Ogeron, whom the Spaniards thought simple-minded, and the surgeon-barber, a man called François la

Faverye, who had done a good turn to a Spaniard and so was allowed to move about freely. He always accompanied M. d'Ogeron in the fields, romping about as people sometimes do with a simpleton, so that the Spaniards themselves were amused to see their antics.

Meanwhile, d'Ogeron and the barber were busy plotting the best way to escape. Eventually they decided to go down to the shore, make a raft and sail over to the island of Santa Cruz – which belongs to the French and lies off the eastern point of Puerto Rico, about ten leagues south-west by east. Having agreed on this plan and promised to stand by each other, they warned the prisoners of their intention and began their journey. All they had was a chopping-knife or machete, which they'd managed to steal from the Spaniards.

They marched a whole day through the forest before they reached the shore. Here they looked out for something suitable for making a raft, but it was long before they found anything which would do. Hunger began to torment them, for there was nothing on the beach to satisfy their appetite, as there had been in the woods with the fruits from the trees.

Necessity is the mother of invention, and the two fugitives were alert for every possible means of getting food. They saw huge shoals of fish, of the kind the Spanish call *corlabados*, close inshore, hunting smaller fish for their prey. Some of these little fish, in the impetus of flight, leapt right out on to the dry sand. D'Ogeron and his comrade succeeded in catching some of the biggest, and even managed to catch some of the predatory *corlabados* as well. Soon they had as many as they could eat, and roasted some for next day as well. They were not at a loss for making a fire: if you rub two sticks together for a quarter of an hour, you can kindle a fire directly. The fugitives took their fish into the woods to cook, for they dared not linger on the beach for fear of being captured again, when they would certainly have been put to death.

While they were busy searching out suitable timber for

their raft, they noticed a small canoe approaching. As it came nearer, they could see there were only two men aboard, whom they guessed were fishermen. D'Ogeron and his companion determined to try and get possession of the canoe, if it should cost them their lives, and hid among the trees close where the boat would come ashore.

Two fishermen got out – one a Spaniard and the other a mulatto. Apparently they had come to fetch water and to go fishing at night among the rocks, for the mulatto at once set off with several small calabashes towards a spring of fresh water not far away. The fugitives sprang on him and clove his head in with their machete. Then they crept up to the Spaniard, who was busy laying out fishing tackle by the canoe, and straight away finished him off too.

They dragged down the other corpse so they could carry both bodies out to sea, to leave no evidence behind for the Spaniards to find. Then they fetched as much fresh water as the boat would carry and immediately sailed to a small sheltered inlet to await the night. No sooner had darkness fallen than they began travelling along the coast of Puerto Rico as far as Cabo Roxo, and from there steered to Hispaniola. Wind and weather were so favourable that in a few days they reached Samana, a cape on the east of that island, where they found their own people.

D'Ogeron sent the barber along the coast to gather all the men he could, while he himself went to Tortuga. Here he sent word to the ships lying in the roads of his intention of liberating the French prisoners, holding out moreover the prospect of good booty, to give them more encouragement. The barber had spread a similar message to the French along the coast of Hispaniola, so that soon he had assembled a good number of men.

D'Ogeron now came sailing along the coast with the numerous ships and men he had gathered together, to pick up the barber's contingent. He urged them to avenge the inhuman cruelties the Spaniards had inflicted on their fellows, and they promised unanimously to follow where he should lead them, expressing great sympathy for the sufferings of their companions at the hands of the Spaniards.

Assured of his men's hearty support, d'Ogeron steered for Puerto Rico. When the island came in sight, the ships used only their lower sails, so the Spaniards would not discover them until they reached the intended landing-place. This caution proved of no avail, however, for the Spaniards had been warned of their approach, and had several companies of horsemen ranging the shore on the look-out. D'Ogeron therefore judged it best to waste no time, and as soon as he had warned his fleet to make ready, came as close inshore as possible and began putting up a heavy covering fire so that his men could quickly land and assail the enemy with unexpected fury.

But events turned out otherwise. The Spaniards hid in the woods, lying flat on their bellies and keeping perfectly still all the time the shooting went on from the ships. Then, when the Frenchmen began entering the forest, the Spaniards made a sudden surprise attack and soon overcame them. The French were forced to retreat to their ships as best they could, leaving many dead and wounded behind them.

M. d'Ogeron managed to save his life, although he was half dead with grief. His attempt had failed, and the men left behind in the hands of these barbarous people would have to pay for it. However, there was no means of liberating them now, for he was too weak and his men panic-stricken. The beach where they had landed gave all the advantage to the defenders, so that one man on shore was as good as ten would-be invaders. Moreover, the Spanish forces had been disproportionately greater than d'Ogeron's. The French were obliged to leave without accomplishing their aim.

The Spaniards stayed on shore until d'Ogeron's ships were out of sight, then they killed off the wounded, cutting off nose and ears from the corpses to take back and show the other prisoners, as a sign of the victory they had won. They prepared a great feast, lit triumphant bonfires and held a tournament, jousting on horseback with their lances at the bound victims dangling from the trees, with a prize for the best aim. Roast meat was set before the starving prisoners, and when they tried to pick up the food, the Spaniards struck at their hands with machetes. Sometimes they would throw bones to the captives, for them to gnaw like dogs, and when the prisoners did not snatch them up, said they could not be very hungry.

Mijnheer Jacob Binkes, vice-admiral of the Dutch fleet, happened to put in at Puerto Rico for provisions and was a witness of this inhumanity. He had the compassion to rescue five or six of the wretched prisoners and take them back to Holland. When the Spaniards found out, they sent the rest of the captives to the capital, where they were employed carrying lime and stones for some fortifications under repair. Then the French prisoners began to pluck up courage a little, for although they had to work like slaves, it seemed their lives would be spared, and they hoped at some time or other to be able to escape.

When the forts had been rebuilt and there was no more work to do in the town, the governor sent the prisoners to Havana, where they were similarly employed. But here they were guarded more strictly, for at the end of their day's work they were put in irons and locked up. The governor feared they might spy out the city's defences, and if they ever got back to their own people use the information to lead an attack on the city, as had often been attempted. For this reason the governor looked out for opportunities of transporting them to Spain. Whenever a ship called in from New Spain on the way back to Europe, two or three Frenchmen were taken aboard to replace sailors who had died or run away. This was what the Frenchmen longed for, praising God for delivering them from their slavery.

Before long they had all been sent to Spain, where they managed to get together and make their way to France, and then looked out for the first chance of returning to Tortuga. They helped one another all they could, those who had money sharing with those who had none. Some who could not forget their sufferings had special knives and pincers made, vowing if they got hold of a Spaniard to flay him alive and tear out his flesh.

Back they came to Tortuga on the first ship they could find. Many went out marauding again, with a fleet then being equipped in Tortuga under the command of M. de Maintenon. They took the island of Trinidad, which lies between Tobago and the coast of Paria, and put it to ransom. Afterwards, their intention was to raid and plunder the city of Caracas, situated nearly opposite Curaçao.

*Some other Penguin Classics are described
on the following pages*

Penguin Classics

ZÁRATE
THE DISCOVERY
AND CONQUEST OF PERU

TRANSLATED BY J. M. COHEN

There is no full eye-witness account of the Spaniards'
dramatic defeat of the Incas. For this new compilation,
therefore, J. M. Cohen has translated the best contemporary history – that of Agustin de Zárate – and
embellished it with first-hand descriptions of the country
and the extraordinary exploits of the conquistadors. These
graphic additions turn Zárate's history, with its careful
record of the discovery and conquest of Peru and of the
subsequent civil wars, into a rounded and continuous
narrative which does justice to the landings, the heroic
marches across the mountains, Atahuallpa's death, and
the incredible harvest of treasure.

Penguin Classics

BERNAL DÍAZ
THE CONQUEST OF
NEW SPAIN

TRANSLATED BY J. M. COHEN

The defeat of the Aztecs by Hernan Cortes and his small band of adventurers is one of the most startling military feats in history. Fifty years after the event Bernal Díaz (*c.* 1498–*c.* 1580), who served under Cortes, wrote this magnificent account of the march from the coast, Montezuma's death, the massacre of the Spaniards, and the eventual capture of the capital of Mexico.

This new translation of a work on which W. H. Prescott drew freely for his *History of the Conquest of Mexico* has been made by J. M. Cohen, the translator of *Don Quixote* and other Penguin Classics.

Penguin Classics

THE VINLAND SAGAS
THE NORSE DISCOVERY
OF AMERICA

TRANSLATED BY MAGNUS MAGNUSSON
AND HERMANN PÁLSSON

The two medieval Icelandic sagas translated in this volume tell one of the most fascinating stories in the history of exploration – the discovery of America by Norsemen, five centuries before Christopher Columbus. In spare and vigorous prose they record Europe's first surprised glimpse of the eastern shores of the North American continent and the Red Indian natives who inhabited them. The Sagas describe how Eirik the Red founded an Icelandic colony in Greenland and how his son, Leif the Lucky, later sailed south to explore and, if possible, exploit the chance discovery by Bjarni Herjolfsson, of an unknown land.

THE PENGUIN CLASSICS

The Most Recent Volumes